Diplomacy and International Law in Globalized Relations

Wilfried Bolewski

Diplomacy and International Law in Globalized Relations

Springer

Ambassador
Dr. Wilfried Bolewski
Foreign Service Academy
German Foreign Office
Schwarzer Weg 45
13505 Berlin, Germany
wilfried.bolewski@diplo.de

Library of Congress Control Number: 2007924089

ISBN 978-3-540-71100-1 Springer Berlin Heidelberg New York

Springer is a part of Springer Science+Business Media

springer.com

Production: LE-TEX Jelonek, Schmidt & Vöckler GbR, Leipzig
Cover-design: WMX Design GmbH, Heidelberg

SPIN 12025053 64/3100YL - 5 4 3 2 1 0 Printed on acid-free paper

Table of Contents

Introduction:
Practitioner's perspective of diplomacy

"In a world where war is everybody's tragedy and everybody's nightmare, diplomacy is everybody's business."

Lord Strang, former British diplomat, 1966

Diplomacy in the 21st century is transforming and expanding from a peaceful method of inter – state relations to a general instrument of communication among globalized societies. Originally, it was practised only by professional diplomats as statecraft. Today, due to the growing number of participants in international relations (States, International Organizations, Non-Governmental Organizations, transnational companies, media, academia and others) the focus of traditional diplomacy is widening, the monopoly on diplomacy by professional diplomats is fading.

Nevertheless, it is their life-long practical experience and professionalism together with learned writings of theorists[1] which form the core of the diplomatic art and skills.

Though diplomatic theory and practice draws on insights from all political and social sciences and humanities (law, politics, economics, culture, philosophy, languages and the arts) it has not yet properly been claimed by any of them. In spite of the multidisciplinary nature of diplomacy it has remained – for a long time – a neglected field of academic study even within the social science of International Relations. No area of world politics has reflected a greater gap between experience and theory than diplomatic statecraft.

Only over the last ten years, academia has discovered diplomacy as a subject of interdisciplinary research[2] Specialized research centres in Europe, the United States and, recently, in Australia are undertaking academic studies in diplomacy. Universities world-wide are opening their curricula to this new field of study, a resurgence of interest in diplomacy is the consequence.

The reasons for neglect in the past may lay in the absence of practical experience for an academic outsider and the lack of analytical and multidisciplinary approach by diplomatic practitioners: This book is an attempt to combine the experience gained from a professional diplomatic career (9 postings in five continents) with the findings of an interdisciplinary research seminar in "diplomatic practice" organized by the Free University of Berlin in cooperation with the German Foreign Office's Special Representative for Universities and Foundations. The choice of topics in this book has been determined by their essential importance for practical diplomacy as experienced by the author as a senior diplomat. In Protocol, this included the organization and accompaniment of visits at the highest level by Presidents, Heads of State and Foreign Ministers. This book is therefore not meant to substitute the exhaustive agenda of a complete Manual on Diplomacy but should be read as a practical supplement. The selected topics treated in this book should serve as general guidelines and facilitate the understanding of underlying principles, structures, currents and developments in today's diplomacy. Combining empirical and theoretical approaches it nevertheless introduces innovative thoughts and terminology for tried and tested structures and new tendencies and perspectives. This study intends to add an actual insider-view from a serving practitioner to current intellectual discussions (in English, French and German) by theorists/academics (whether political scientists, legal experts or historians) on contemporary diplomatic methods and problems.

Practising diplomats have little time for extensive reading of academic work, and most theorists have inadequate notions of the actual work performed by diplomats in real time live settings and their accelerating complexity. One immediate consequence is that outstanding concepts developed by astute theory analysts, especially those that are in relative proximity to diplomacy practised on the ground, do not reach the practitioner audience. The latter would gain by relating their experience to such theory, and use the lessons offered to sharpen their skills.[3]

The content of this study centres on the changing role of diplomacy due to the increasing number of globalized participants. This study could thereby bridge the academia – policy gap and stimulate more interest and research in diplomacy as a field of academic study.

Diplomacy needs to draw on interdisciplinary and international research to cope with new problems and unpredictable missions thereby exploiting the crossroads between diplomacy and socially responsible sciences. The impact of science upon diplomacy as a social reality has yet to be explored in our time.[4]

New problems affecting diplomacy are manifold: international terrorism, religious or ethnically motivated conflicts, economic and social upheaval, illegal migration, environmental or natural catastrophes, failing states, international crime and corruption to name just a few.

The political system of statehood[5] is facing a multitude of challenges due to the increasing number of international contacts as well as the momentum and complexity of problem solutions. The social, economic and political framework for state activities is changing. The state as an institution can still demonstrate and activate considerable forces for unity and problem-solving within its community but its inherent advantage of information and the monopoly of decision seems to be waning.

With changing demands on the state the contours of statehood are shifting. Some even call it a decline of the role of the state. But this critique overlooks the fact that increased transnational cooperation and innovative forms of political coordination create new forms and spheres of activity and efficacy which potentially can contribute to the reestablishment of state competences. States can grow stronger through cooperative partnerships with non-state participants. This indeed presupposes that they adjust their self-understanding from subordination to coordination in order to support or even initiate processes of civil organizations.

States and national governments can no longer assume to be the sole locus of effective political power. This power is now shared and apportioned by diverse forces (entities, agencies and even individuals) at the national, transnational and regional level including governments, civil society organizations and transnational corporations. They are creating arenas for debate, consultations and formation of political decision-making. This involves a spread of layers of regional and global political governance. Global politics and multilayered governance are thus challenging the efficacy of national democratic traditions and institutions. A new definition of participatory democracy and the admission of legitimate political activities by self-regulating associations must eventually allow all stake-holders to access to political processes alongside nation-states. Democracy must become a feature of the multiple interactions of networks and decision-making fora.[6]

There is no doubt a need to transform international cooperation from its traditional place as external affairs into policy-making applicable to most, if not all, domestic issue areas. Thus, the state system needs adjustment. If private groups in society step in to carry out services and tasks that originally belong to the state (for example supply of food, water, housing, energy, health, education, transport, security) the crucial question of the genuine core functions of the modern state comes to the fore, those inherent responsibilities that cannot be outsourced, delegated or privatized by the state.

On the basis of the monopoly of the state to use force these should comprise – as a minimum definition of the state as the guarantor of the public weal – the guarantee of internal and external public security, law and order and the freedom for its citizens.

The core task and concern of any foreign ministry is the coordination of a coherent foreign policy through diplomacy ("Kohärenzkompetenz"). Politics and diplomacy have not lost their abilities actively to shape decisions necessary for the community but they have to justify their state of the art capability and thereby their legitimacy for community problem-solving through modern means and methods. Politics and diplomacy thus move more and more towards a "learning system" which not only finds but controls and corrects its decisions on the basis of competence.

Good governance depends to a large extent on good advice being injected into the governance process to help guide key decision makers with regard to the quality of the decisions taken and policies adopted in order to produce outcomes that are broadly efficient, equitable, sustainable, and cost effective. Policy advice can help to outline just how serious a problem is and elucidate the causes of that problem in a way that sets the parameters for governmental action. As policy responses to a problem are being formulated, policy expertise with its constant flow of new ideas and concepts can be critical in identifying the most important alternatives, evaluating their advantages and disadvantages. There is a growing demand for expert advice in politics because it is seen to be less partial and more imaginative and because the growing complexity of government requires specialized forms of expertise not typically resident in government bureaucracies. On the other hand, supply of such advice is growing as academia and groups within civil society establish their own sources of expertise to assess government initiatives and influence them with their own recommendations.[7]

Diplomacy can and should learn from academia in the field of expertise, political-moral values and the assessment of consequences. Politics requires a constant flow of new ideas and concepts if it is to master the urgent and complex problems that face it today. Public policy now relies heavily on social scientists for input. Modern science can secure political-moral values. Its international nature exemplifies the transition of national borders.

In order to find practicable solutions to institutional and existential problems caused by accelerating globalization diplomacy needs interdisciplinary guidance by social sciences. Applied human sciences thus take on the meaning of practice-orientated science.

The relationship between science and society, including government, is changing through an increasing process of communication and open dialogue.[8] The objective is to construct a climate of reciprocal knowledge and trust. Today, public engagement of science is to be seen as an obligation, not a luxury. One of the social sciences' most important cultural contributions is its example as good training for democracy. Society needs science for political, social and economic success. Science has to open up to responsibility and accountability towards society in a new "contrat social", in which scientists' work finds its adequate maximization.

With the pursuance and dissemination of knowledge as a human resource comes responsibility. Experts are no longer distant bearers of relevant knowledge, but assume some kind of responsibility for their recommendations.[9] Science today has to face up to its social responsibility just as business is accepting it on a voluntary basis. Traditional freedom of research, together with business commitment, should be moulded by the state into a new public/private partnership. Thus, a constructive triad of responsibility would emerge: state/business/science (academia). Such involvement of modern science is an expression of a participatory democracy and a politically responsible civil society and could provide innovative ideas and dynamics and even early breakthrough thinking leading possibly towards tectonic shifts or time-breaks. Such solutions to good governance through testing in political life can prove profitable to the community as a whole. For this purpose, the transparency from academia to politics has to be improved fundamentally.

Good policy-making cannot take place in a vacuum; it has to be based on adequate information and assessment. Governments should rely on the views of different protagonists such as its own departments as well as the scientific community. For a broader base of decision-making governments face the problem of bringing expert knowledge to bear in their political decision making including alternatives, costs, implications and consequences. Governments should make use of the potential of ideas and multidisciplinary solutions to transnational problems (as created by globalization) produced in universities and think tanks as a form of intellectual diplomacy[10] before others impose their political priorities and societal choices. There is also a clear need for an international approach to science policy ("Außenwissenschaftspolitik", "diplomatie intellectuelle").

The complexity and unpredictability of modern government, the growing diversification and complexity of participants and issues, the speed of communication, the growing size of available information, the increased workload imposed on diplomats by these developments all tend to limit the time and resources available for policy analysis and formulation. No administration has the means, man-power or time for the necessary medium to long-term, deep-rooted, wide-spread, non-hierarchical, independent and imaginative reflection and analysis as these laboratories of ideas. This complementary source of knowledge should not be seen only as a feature of political fashion but as the consequence of the complexity and the velocity of today's developments. It is through its application that the vitality of democracy can be strengthened in the political process because these policy-thinking organizations (think tanks) provide an integral and important element of the pluralism in civil society in search of excellence.[11] They provide research, analysis and advice on immediate policy concerns with significant autonomy from government and societal interests. In comparison, university-based social scientists, in the past, conducted research relevant to scholarly and theoretically based debates rather than confronting the most current and pressing policy questions of the day.

The applied pluridisciplinary research with innovative, original or alternative solutions and options to international public problems can bridge the interface between academic reflection and political influence and action. We are clearly moving into a progressive "scientification" of the political decision-making process with an international dimension.

In view of the timely and appropriate realization of the coordinating competence by the foreign ministry such political consultancy and advice through academia seems not only very valuable but eventually indispensable in the endeavour to foresee the unexpected and to imagine the future.

This innovative concept presupposes an opening of the foreign ministry towards the civil society comprising the readiness for dialogue within a political learning process. This opening extends from mutual interesting topics to sabbatical exchange of personnel. Foreign policy-making in the future is likely to become more open, to involve more external participants and will stimulate more public debate.

On the other hand it requests a better understanding by civil society including science and academia of the demands, conditions and working processes for political decisions under time-pressure, uncertainty and unpredictability of changing circumstances, future events and developments. Scientists should develop a greater sensitivity to the social and political impact of the advice proffered. The foreign ministry, on the other hand, should carry its external affairs expertise into the civil society via networking in order to foster understanding and support for its work and responsibilities.

In order to coordinate such a partnership the German Foreign Office, for example, has created the position of a Special Representative for Universities and Foundations with the following tasks:

- stock-taking of academic research projects in the field of international relations and diplomacy,
- subsequent comparison with topical global questions under practical review in the foreign ministry and

- initiation of a fruitful dialogue with the aim of political consultancy and sabbatical exchanges.

Among other tasks this Special Representative will administer the support of the German Foreign Ministry for the cluster of excellence on "Governance in a globalized world" under the direction of the Free University of Berlin which could include under the heading of knowledge exchange and dissemination activities:

- Research colleges/graduate schools
- Berlin Governance Forum on constitutionalization beyond the nation state and especially
- a Summer School in Diplomatic Studies in cooperation with the German Foreign Office and the private sector for a true interplay between researchers and practitioners.

Clusters of excellence are part of the Excellence initiative by the German federal and state governments to promote science and research at German universities. Excellence clusters are aimed at setting up internationally visible and competitive research and educational facilities at German universities and promoting the development of scientific networks and collaborations. Each of approximately 30 excellence clusters can receive an average of 6.5 million euros per year.

All sides will profit from this triangular partnership. With regard to science the insights of practising diplomats may lead to up-to-date academic teaching and quality empirical research.

This realistic linkage between academia and practise necessitates an early exposure by students of international relations already at university level to topics of diplomatic practice. This not only in view of a learned assessment for approaching a proper diplomatic career but for any activity in extended international relations (administration, IOs, NGOs, media, transnational enterprises, academia etc.)

Experienced (serving or former) diplomats in residence can provide the impetus to knowledge transfer and exchange through disseminating activities, thus realistically qualifying students for a broader international career.

Mutual sabbatical exchanges between universities, research institutes and think tanks on one side and government agencies on the other could create and support multiple synergies and capacities from problem-orientated basic research to practical policy consultancy.

Summer Schools in Diplomatic Studies in cooperation with the foreign ministry should invite academics and professional diplomats to teach students in diplomacy as an international practice and to prepare them to meet global challenges that transcend borders, disciplines and policy sectors by offering professional education for broader international careers.

References

1 **G.R. Berridge/Maurice Keens-Soper/T.G. Otte**, Diplomatic Theory from Machiavelli to Kissinger (Basingstoke: Palgrave, 2001) Studies in Diplomacy;
G.R. Berridge, Diplomatic Classics: Selected texts from Commynes to Vattel (Basingstoke: Palgrave Macmillan 2004);
Christer Jönsson/Richard Langhorne, Diplomacy (London: Sage Publications, 2004), vol. I-III.

2 Some recent reference books on diplomacy:
G.R. Berridge (with Alan James), A Dictionary of Diplomacy (Basingstoke: Palgrave Macmillan, 2003), 2nd.ed.;
G.R. Berridge, Diplomacy: theory and practice, (Basingstoke: Palgrave Macmillan 2005) 3rd. ed.;
Jan Melissen (ed.), Innovation in diplomatic practice (London: Macmillan 1999) Studies in Diplomacy;
Christer Jönsson/Martin Hall, Essence of Diplomacy (Houndmills: Palgrave Macmillan 2005), Studies in Diplomacy and International Relations;
Keith Hamilton/Richard Langhorne, The Practice of Diplomacy (London/New York: Routlege 1995);
Kishan S. Rana, Inside Diplomacy (New Delhi: Manas Publications 2002) revised edition;
Samy Cohen, Les diplomates: Négocier dans un monde chaotique (Paris: Autrement 2002);
Alain Plantey, Principes de diplomatie (Paris: Editions A. Pedone 2002);
Guillaume Devin, Sociologie des relations internationales (Paris: La Découverte 2002).

3 **Kishan S. Rana**, Inside Diplomacy, p. 442.

4 **Gunther Hellmann (ed.),** Forschung und Beratung in der Wissensgesellschaft. Das Feld der internationalen Beziehungen und der Außenpolitik (Baden-Baden: Nomos Verlagsgesellschaft 2007);
Svenja Falk/Dieter Rehfeld/Andrea Römmele/Martin Thunert (ed.), Handbuch Politikberatung (Wiesbaden: Verlag für Sozialwissenschaften 2006)

5 **Stephan Leibfried/Michael Zürn (ed.),** Transformation of the State? (Cambridge: Cambridge University Press 2005).

6 **Giovanni Carrada**, Communicating Science: A scientist's survival kit (Luxembourg: Office for Official Publications of the European Communities, 2006) http://ec.europa.eu/research/science-society/pdf/communicating-science_ eu.pdf.

7 **Martin W. Thunert**, Germany, in: **R. Kent Weaver/Paul B. Stares (ed.),** Guidance for governance. Comparing alternative sources of public policy advice, (Tokyo: Japan Center for International Exchange 2001) p. 157 (199)

[8] **Stephen Boucher/Martine Royo**, Les Think Tanks: cerveaux de la guerre des idées, (Paris: Editions du Félin 2006).

[9] **Martin W. Thunert**, Germany, **in: R. Kent Weaver/Paul B. Stares (ed.),** Guidance for governance. Comparing alternative sources of public policy advice, p. 157 (199)

[10] **James McGann/R. Kent Weaver (ed.),** Think Tanks and Civil Societies: Catalysts for ideals and action (New Jersey: Transaction Publishers 2000);
James McGann, Les laboratoires d'idées et la transnationalisation de la politique étrangère (Foreign Policy Research Institute, 2002, http://usinfo.state.gov/journals/itps/1102/ijpf/frmcgann.htm).

[11] **Wolfgang H. Reinicke**, Tugging at the sleeves of politicians. Think tanks – American expericences and German perspectives, (Gütersloh: Bertelsmann Foundation Publishers 1996)

Part I
Essentials of modern diplomacy

Traditional diplomacy is practised as the art and craft of communicating and interchanging among states acting through their representatives (diplomats) in the national interest (be it political, economic, scientific, social or other) by peaceful means. These means do not exclude the use of (political or economic) pressure (short of war) which is defined as coercive diplomacy. Raymond Aron already distinguished between "L'art de convaincre" and "L'art de contraindre".[1]

The difference between diplomacy and foreign policy is related to that of instruments (of execution) and of formulation and contents of policy. Diplomacy as a method deals with the articulation of foreign policy. It is about the means, not the ends, of foreign policy. Diplomacy thus serves as an instrument of implementing foreign policy. International relations on the other hand is the social science of analysing foreign policy. International relations deal with relations between states, while transnational relations concern transboundary interactions in which at least one societal actor is involved.

Diplomacy uses a certain set of skills, tools, procedures, methods, norms and rules as social practises in order to orchestrate and moderate the dialogue between states and thus to optimize the content and quality of international relations, including the management of change.

The universally recognized legal frameworks for these practices are the Vienna Convention on Diplomatic Relations (1961) and the Vienna Convention on Consular Relations (1963) as well as customary international law. An important part of these rules are made up of protocol as the guideline for orderly official or representational behaviour of diplomats. These instruments of diplomatic interchange are either verbal or written.

The most common form of written communication is the Verbal Note (Note Verbale) informing about a fact or position or initiating/requesting a certain action. The Verbal Note has a standard line of courtesy at the beginning and at the end. The wording of the diplomatic Verbal Note should be courteous, respectful, sober and unemotional. Diplomatic language with its formalisation into special patterns carries a certain subdued tone of understatement. At best, it should also leave a face saving room for the opposing party to respond in kind while protecting the messenger from the responsibility of its impact.

In conference diplomacy there are contrasting roles of ambiguity and precision: weaker parties may have an interest in inserting ambiguous provisions, while stronger partners will push for precision. The precision of the wording may (at times deliberately) be clouded by some ambiguity to retain flexibility and the ability to disclaim. This then can lead to different interpretations. Ambiguity allows participants to issue signals they can later disown and gives them more freedom to explore possible policies without changing others' images of themselves to their detriment. The advantages of this often outweigh the disadvantages and many techniques of signalling are adopted to utilize these potentialities.[2] In diplomacy, ambiguity is a central and constructive practice since it creates the necessary room to manoeuvre and momentum for transaction and compromise.[3]

The verbal communication in diplomatic contacts should follow the same lines respecting the institution of (recognized) states and International Organizations, the sovereignty and equality of states (small or large) as well as the dignity of its representatives. The main feature of any communication among human beings including diplomats is trustworthiness, credibility and integrity. In matters of state it is essential to build up and maintain a high level of respectability with your counterparts as well as other official contacts for the enduring success of your mission and your whole diplomatic career.

A caveat for joking diplomats: At times, a joke may generate an awareness of the shared assumptions uniting all members beyond the barriers of cultural divisions. But, any diplomatic joke should be amusing for all and offending to none. The due respect for other cultures may demand necessary adjustments or avoidance altogether.

All diplomats are agents of their state and do not act as private citizens. They have to fulfil an official mission regardless of their personal opinion. The imperative mandate of a diplomat who disagrees with his government's policy forces him, in case of unsuccessful remonstration, to defend his Government's position loyally or to resign from his mission.

Some of the salient features of change impacting on diplomacy are:

1. Acceleration of globalization
2. New participants in globalized relations
3. New information techniques
4. Internationalization of domestic politics.

Ad 1: Acceleration of globalization

Contemporary globalization is creating a world where the extensive reach of transnational relations and networks is matched by their high intensity, velocity, and impact propensity across many facets of life, from economic and social to environmental. In a changing global environment the network of international relations is strengthening in all and even new fields of politics, economy and social contacts. Globalization is a process of economic, political and cultural convergence or homogenisation. It can be defined by the following four elements:

- Global challenges demanding governmental, intergovernmental or private solutions
- Intensification of political and economic integration
- Increase in the number of transnational participants and issues
- Technological leap facilitating new working methods.

Globalization poses a series of new practical questions:

- How can effective and legitimate governance be sustained in interdependent global, regional, national, and local spaces?
- Which legal, political, economic, social, and cultural problems and conflicts emerge, and how can they be dealt with?
- How can governance at the various levels cope with economic globalization, social fragmentation, and heterogeneous cultures and traditions?
- Which socio-cultural prerequisites are needed for a global world order and effective global governance beyond the nation-state in view of increasing ethnic, cultural, and religious divisions?
- How can we develop a systematic understanding of the emergence of, and solutions to, long-term and inter-generational policy problems?

Globalization refers to processes of social, economic, and cultural change that systematically reduce the significance of national societies in favour of intensified transboundary interactions on all levels. Globalization vastly increases our exposure to other participants, spaces, and environments.

Ad 2: New participants in globalized relations

Whereas the traditional participants in international relations were limited to states and International Organizations (as original subjects in international law) a growing number of participants has emerged due to the globalization process: Sub state entities (local and regional) NGOs, transnational companies, the media, academia, foundations, political parties etc.). Today, foreign policy in a larger sense is not only performed by states through their representatives but also by any of these new participants. The practice of diplomacy is shared with many more partners than before. Diplomacy has become privatized and popularized.

In the future, the sovereign state is unlikely to remain the main locus of authority. New constellations and participants are transcending the divide between the domestic and the international spheres replacing old forms of governance. While the sovereign state is likely to structurally remain the principal source of authority due to its structural endurance and normative relevance the principle of sovereignty will undergo profound changes leading to a modernized concept. Sovereignty today is not any more monopolized by the state, but – through changes across time and space – can be divided and shared among state and non-state participants depending on the issue, problem and political situation of the community.[4] Due to these internal challenges to state sovereignty at sub-national levels of governance, sovereignty as relational interface between law and politics has become a continuous variable. Thus, sovereignty is transferred and relocated in some issue areas to other levels than state entities.

Governance has been recognized (by the Report of the Commission on Global Governance in 1995) as the sum of the many ways indiviuals and institutions, public and private, manage their common affairs.

The new modes of governance must lead to adjustments in constitutional provisions to ensure legitimacy and accountability as well as the rule of law. The rule of law means that the exercise of political power is permissible only on the basis of the constitution and of laws whose form and substance complies with the constitution, and with a view to ensuring human dignity, freedom, justice and legal certainty. Such constitutionalism is an indispensable normative frame for thinking about the complex problems of viable and legitimate regulation of the transboundary communities. Legitimacy is meant to be the morally justifiable and acceptable exercise of political power. The conditions of progressive internationalization are impacting on the new political culture and its acceptance and will entail a reduction in the standards and expectations of legitimacy (legitimacy-deficit), certainly for the private authority.

The new participants are capable of prejudicing and possibly binding the position of the state to varying degrees. The foreign ministries no longer play a role of gatekeepers in external affairs but can at best become coordinators. Depending on the form, time and content of the external actions of other participants this can be a blessing or a curse for any coordination of policy by the foreign ministry. The internal and external coordination function is not an entirely new preoccupation, but it has become more central since it involves simultaneous operations in different public and private arenas in search for a unified voice on policy matters.

Ad 3: New information technologies

The new information technologies will not usurp the rationale for diplomacy and for diplomats.[5] Diplomacy, by its very nature, is an ongoing process which does not lend itself easily to short-termism. Diplomacy requires knowledge, judgement, and expertise. Negotiating over the Internet does not change that. It just demands adaptation to the world around us. This adaptation is not a matter of choice but of necessity. Technology is having an impact, not only on how diplomats do business, but on what the business of diplomacy is.

New information techniques have improved not only the speed but also the depth of available material. This also affects diplomacy as the art of communicating and interacting among the participants in globalized relations. This communication evolution has not only accelerated the flow of information but has also broadened the mentality and the ways of thinking within the diplomatic community. Reaction time has unavoidably shortened in this dialogue. A diplomat can seldom beat the modern media in velocity but he is constantly challenged to analyse the events with the in-depth quality and continuity of his special and wide-spread sources which can influence domestic opinion as well as the policy formulating process at home.

In the future, a diplomat will be assessed by the depth and specificity of the detailed information and the critical analysis he provides. Thereby he should be able to foresee in the medium as well as long term social and political trends which can be dealt with at an early stage through public diplomacy.

In spite of any new technology such as e-mail, fax or telephone nothing can really replace a personal contact and dialogue confirmed by a handshake.

On the other hand any diplomatic initiative and activity on the ground can be constantly monitored by his administration at home which is able to provide more detailed and frequent and even real-time instructions according to domestic interests.

Ad 4: Internationalization of domestic politics

Due to advancing globalization and the increase in transnational relations and interdependencies foreign policy today is not only formulated in the foreign ministry but in other ministries and agencies with international contacts (administrative diversification of foreign policy). In as much as other departments according to their domestic competences are developing their own international networks (epistemic community) and obtaining concomitant decision-making power a process of internationalization of domestic politics and domesticating of international relations is emanating. Thus the diplomat abroad may be confronted at times with multiple chains of principals representing differing interests and giving varying instructions. In order to secure that the government consistently and coherently speaks with one voice in matters of foreign policy it is the task of the diplomat to find a consolidated position respecting the primacy of the foreign ministry as the coordinating authority.[6] The foreign ministry itself might use inter-ministerial working groups to co-ordinate government policy. On the international level, other ministries are also participating in regular (bilateral/trilateral) government to government consultations.

This coordinating role of the foreign ministry in matters of foreign policy is challenged by the multitude of co-participants in international relations. Since the state has lost its monopoly on information and decision making in this field it has to regain its capacity and credibility to shape foreign policy on a daily basis. This can be achieved if (foreign) policy making is understood as a "learning system" for decisions, their control and correction. Foreign policy can learn a lot from international social sciences with regard to political-moral expertise and the assessment of the consequences. Social sciences can provide valuable historic and multidisciplinary insights and analyses to facilitate the decision making process by the diplomats. Practice-orientated science can contribute to the solutions of many institutional as well as existential problems created by the transformation of statehood.

Similar to business science takes on a social responsibility towards the state and civil society in a public-private-partnership. Political consultancy through the sciences is not only desirable but it becomes existential. Progress in science also opens new fields of activity and perspectives to diplomacy.

In consequence, the practical roles of a diplomat have changed. His traditional mission used to be:

Representation and promotion of state interests (political, economic, cultural, scientific and others)
Protection of citizens-interest
Negotiation
Gathering and transmitting of information.

Today, additional tasks come to the fore:

Project manager
Moderator
Multiplier (public diplomacy)
Analyst
Conceptional thinker
Crisis manager

A modern diplomat is involved in cultural, scientific, development, human aid as well as environmental projects. In case of natural or man-made disasters he takes on the role of crises management coordinating the interests of his state and citizens on the ground.

In practical terms the diplomat is seen as the first mediator and moderator of interests between the sending and the receiving state.

In an age of globally interlinked media, diplomacy must go beyond the traditional forms of state-to-state relations. A modern foreign service will increasingly find itself directly addressing the broader public.

With the technology-leap in information public diplomacy has taken on a new significance. Public diplomacy is defined as the sum of all communication activities directed towards selected elite, contact organizations, and the broader public worldwide. The long-term goal is to modernize and revitalize a country's image and thereby make it more attractive for partners, investors, consumers, and tourists. In addition, public diplomacy helps to explain current domestic and foreign policy to a worldwide audience in an understandable manner, resulting in increased support for national positions.

Public diplomacy, thus, deals with the influence of public opinions and attitudes towards the formation and execution of foreign policies. Public diplomacy, therefore, is about getting people on one's side. It concerns the relationship between diplomats and foreign societies, particularly multipliers of opinions in those societies, and the facilitation by diplomats of the relationship between people in their own civil society with their counterparts in the receiving state.[7] Today's diplomat has the personal task to explain and defend all aspects of life in his country with all modern means in a proactive and convincing way. This cross-medial communication should be geared in a credible and convincing way towards specific audiences (for example political, economic or cultural decision makers, elites, journalists, students or youth as multipliers) aiming at sustainable effects of informing and opinion-building.

American diplomacy in the 21st century is planning to advance public diplomacy into transformational diplomacy in order to localize the diplomatic posture.[8] Out of the need to enhance the ability to work more effectively at the critical intersections of diplomacy, democracy promotion, economic reconstruction and military security, transformational diplomacy requires to move the diplomatic presence out of foreign capitals and to spread it more widely across countries. A more economical idea than to build new consulates is tested (in Egypt and Indonesia): American Presence Posts. A diplomat moves outside the embassy to live and work and represent his country in an emerging community of change and to engage with private citizens in regional centers. Another way to adopt a more local posture is through a Virtual Presence Post: a young diplomatic officer creates and manages an internet site (Net Diplomacy) that is focused on key population centers. In digital meeting rooms foreign (mostly young) citizens can engage online with American diplomats in embassies or consulates. This system seems to be feasible for spread out areas of Asia and Latin America.

With modern means of communication, information – whether true or false, verifiable or not – is readily available in abundance at any place and any time. The genuine task of today's diplomat lies in scrutinising and analysing the sources, content and credibility of all available facts and opinions. This diplomatic analysis should put the facts into a broader and deeper political context. Thus it could provide an appropriate background assessment and guideline for decisions by his foreign ministry.

On the basis of his long-standing and far-reaching background knowledge as well as his continuous presence, normally for 3-5 years, the diplomat can eventually prove himself as a conceptional thinker providing to his principals exclusive proposals for future-orientated policy guidance.

In order to master the complexity and acceleration of change in globalized relations any participant has to find structural guidance in the following dominant features of modern diplomacy, its procedures and dynamics as they have been experienced by a practitioner:

- internalization of diplomacy versus internationalization of domestic policy
- symbolism and rituals in diplomacy
- flexibility and pragmatism as response to global challenges
- reciprocity versus communitarianism
- corporate diplomacy
- diplomatic culture and the relevance of language
- diplomacy as an instrument of globalized societies

References

[1] **Raymond Aron,** Paix et guerre entre les nations (Paris: Calmann-Lévy 1962), p. 68

[2] **Robert Jervis**, The logic of images in international relations, (Princeton: Princeton University Press 1970), p. 138
Robert Jervis, Perception and misperception in international politics (Princeton: Princeton University Press 1976)

[3] **Constance Villar,** Le discours diplomatique, (Paris: L'Harmattan 2006), p. 235

[4] **Jens Bartelson,** The concept of sovereignty revisited, in: European Journal of International Law, vol. 17 (2006), No. 2, p. 463

[5] **Richard Grant,** The democratisation of diplomacy: negotiating with the Internet, Oxford Internet Institute, Research Report No. 5, November 2004

[6] For the US see:
Strobe Talbott, Globalization and Diplomacy: A Practitioner's Perspective, in: Foreign Policy, 108 (1997), p. 69
For Germany see:
Walter Eberlei/Christopf Weller, Deutsche Ministerien als Akteure von Global Governance. Eine Bestandsaufnahme der auswärtigen Beziehungen der Bundesministerien, Institut für Entwicklung und Frieden der Gerhard-Mercator-Universität Duisburg, INEF Report 52/2001
Lisette Andreae / Karl Kaiser, Die "Außenpolitik" der Fachministerien, in: **Wolf-Dieter Eberweis/Karl Kaiser (ed.)**, Deutschlands neue Außenpolitik, vol. 4: Institutionen und Ressourcen, (München: R. Oldenburg Verlag 1998)

[7] **Jan Melissen (ed.),** The New Public Diplomacy: Soft Power in International Relations, (Houndmills: Palgrave Macmillan 2005), Studies in Diplomacy and International Relations
Joseph S. Nye, Soft Power: The Means of Success in World Politics (New York: Public Affairs 2004)

[8] **Condoleezza Rice** in a speech at the School of Foreign Service at Georgetown University on January 18, 2006 (U.S. Department of State, Fact Sheet: Transformational Diplomacy)

Chapter 1
Diplomacy between statecraft and social science

Diplomacy cannot claim to be a science. In the execution of foreign policy it is practised as statecraft, at best an art. As a profession and social reality it draws from findings of sciences such as social, legal and administrative sciences, psychology, philosophy and others. They all contribute valuable insights and analyses to facilitate the daily task of diplomats. The knowledge of the latest international developments in the social sciences becomes an essential asset among the tools of any diplomat.

The impact of human sciences upon contemporary diplomacy correlates with the influence of modern sciences upon policy making generally. An interdisciplinary academic background is therefore a prerequisite of any future diplomat.

Diplomacy as a profession cannot be learned only from a classical manual, the diplomatic art of human interaction in globalized relations has eventually to be experienced in life through apprenticeship on the job in a foreign ministry and in missions abroad. The methods of diplomacy being taught and experienced are also subject to adaptation within the changing technological environment.

Throughout the centuries diplomacy has proven to be a stabilizing institution in the pursuit of peaceful exchange relations among the states and new participants in globalized relations. When and where necessary it has skilfully adjusted its norms, rules and practices to changing circumstances by adding new layers rather than replacing traditional ones. As the nature of human interaction the genuine character of diplomacy and its timeless methods will survive as a fundamental and primary institution. Therefore, in spite of all changes and adaptations diplomacy as an international institution is not vanishing in globalized relations.

The adapted form of modern diplomacy as an institution and code of conduct can also contribute to the realisation of good governance. Since the role of diplomacy is continuously evolving and expanding with new challenges and participants it now has a chance to also become an appropriate instrument for global good governance. The new common priorities (sustainable peace and development in changing environments, comprehensive security, promotion of human rights and democratic and pluralistic practices, prevention of international terrorism, crime and corruption) could lead to a reinvigorating renaissance of diplomacy.[1] In international relations the awareness of common interests and values beyond national interests is growing. International Organizations and Non-Governmental-Organizations (such as Transparency International) with their regional and global aims and purposes are the testing ground for such humanitarian ideals and values. Very often national governments and their leaders are associating and identifying themselves with these universalistic values or commonly accepted norms in their bilateral and multilateral interactions as "common ground of mankind". Shared knowledge and consensus of underlying principles form the common aim of desirable international standards as part of the concept of global good governance.

Diplomacy's preoccupation with the adaptation of technological advances within its system should not lead to neglect in balancing this development with the promotion of common interests and values. The pursuance of the common good should be given the due attention and importance in diplomatic efforts. It requires a growing sense of community in a common life world (gemeinsame Lebenswelt).[2]

Through its flexibility and adaptability diplomacy will emerge as an instrument for this universal good in the 21st century. Proliferating and polylateral diplomacy may thus contribute to the establishment of global good governance in the interest of the community of mankind.

References

1 **Vladimir Petrovsky**, Diplomacy as an Instrument of Good Governance, http://www.diplomacy.edu/Books/mdiplomacy_book/petrovski/petrovski.htm

2 **Thomas Risse,** Let's Argue!: Communicative Action in World Politics, in: International Organization 54/1, 2000, p.10

Chapter 2
Internalization of diplomacy or internationalization of domestic policy

On the one hand the traditional nation state is transferring powers and competences to supra-national-bodies (like the EU), on the other hand the central government often sees its exclusive foreign policy responsibility undermined from regional governments with considerable devolved powers. Formerly, the ministry of foreign affairs played the role of a gatekeeper vis-à-vis the outside world. But this notion of gateway is too hegemonic because it hinges on the assumption that domestic and international affairs are conducted in two very different political arenas: one within the state's boundaries, the other outside them. It implies exclusive control over the domestic-international interface. In the gobalized situation of state-society and society-society interaction the foreign ministry needs to share or relinquish its gatekeeper status with reference to other participants.[1] With varying degree of constitutional and political independence some of these regional entities are very active in international relations.

As foreign policy – through the interference of other government ministries and agencies – has ceased to be the sole domain of the ministry of foreign affairs one can observe the phenomenon of "degovernmentalization" of foreign affairs by sub-state authorities (provincial, regional or local). In the modern practice of democracy the search for belonging has strengthened collective identities at the regional and local level (regions such as Normandy, Catalonia, and Cornwall). As a reaction to the impact of globalization this development has been called "glocalization".[2]

For the participation of official sub state entities in external actions (for example in the USA, Canada, Belgium, Spain and Germany) the term of "para diplomacy" ("Nebenaussenpolitik")[3] has been coined. Though these sub-state entities do not dispose of the requisite capacities of fully fledged international participants (for example recognition as subjects of international law), in fact their international interactions are becoming increasingly intensive and permanent and thus important in positioning themselves between sovereign states and non-governmental organisations. They very often dispose of an extensive margin of autonomy and numerous resources[4] which might be more sizable than those of a vast majority of sovereign states empowering them with greater influence over international affairs than the central state. Originally these external activities only concerned "soft areas" such as city or regional partnerships, visits of communal delegations, lately they extend to solidarity actions in humanitarian and development aid and effect even core-issues of national representation and foreign policy (economic, political and even military).[5] As cities become centres of economic development their external offices exchange experiences and share interests across national and regional boundaries and develop global economic networks outside the knowledge and influence of traditional diplomats.

In German federalism with its delegation of powers to the European Union the functional and normative dynamics spreading sub-national involvement in international affairs lead to a parallel foreign policy ("Nebenaussenpolitik"). German states ("Länder") act side by side with the federal state level and even set up their separate missions and representations in Brussels. Constitutionally, foreign affairs remain under the responsibility of the federal government but both sides make use of their own diplomacy (micro diplomacy or multilayered diplomacy). This parallelism, at times, can cause frictions in policy matters.

The development of regional networks can pose challenges to traditional diplomatic services by undermining embassies' hegemony over bilateral relations between states. Some of their activities are carried out outside the control or at least without knowledge of the bilateral embassies. They can even cause political and constitutional problems when the central government has to bear the responsibility before supra-national tribunals for international situations created by regional governments.

An extreme form of micro diplomacy by sub-state entities is the pursuance of the political aim of total separation from the federation and its recognition as an independent state called proto-diplomacy.[6]

The growing interdependence and interaction between international and domestic policy is linked together by the internal need for legitimacy and consensual support for these policies at all levels of governance. Putnam[7] talks of a "two level game" in diplomacy which could also be called "intermestic affairs" (mixed international and domestic). This new terminological synthesis points to the reality of growing intertwining of international affairs and domestic policies in globalized relations. It reflects the fact, that globalization has changed the relationship between domestic and world politics and challenged the way in which politics is conducted internationally.

The classical normative and empirical distinctions between the categories "domestic" and "international" and their order of primacy cannot be upheld.[8] Both the domestic and the international settings are in continual transformation. Today, they rather constitute a seamless web with high levels of cooperative interdependence[9] due to the collectivization of objectives. The increasing numbers of international interactions endanger both the coordination and control of foreign affairs by a government and the distinction between foreign and domestic affairs.

The common thread to these practices on the borderline of international and domestic politics is the acceptance that diplomacy as a set of behavioural rules has the capacity to provide a coordinating bridge between the different layers of state and international interaction. Diplomacy is entering new and specialized issue areas (for example environmental diplomacy, human rights diplomacy, trade and financial diplomacy), and domestic policy is becoming more internationalized. Diplomacy is being performed by a growing number of governmental entities as well as new participants such as transnational corporations. These new participants through their own activities then create new diplomatic needs and additional branches of diplomacy such as corporate diplomacy. This may also necessitate consultations between and common training among various participants. Links among participants could be strengthened if national negotiating teams engaged in full consultations before and after international negotiations. The combinations to be brought together may include professional organizations, local and national governments, commercial interests and expert advisers. This becomes the new task of diplomacy. Thus, diplomacy, its procedures and dynamics prove to be the appropriate general instrument at all levels of globalized societies.

References

[1] **Jonathan W. Moses/Torbjorn Knutsen**, Globalization and the reorganization of Foreign affairs ministries, in: Cooperation and conflict (London, Sage Publications 2001) vol. 36 (4), p. 355

[2] **Roland Robertson,** Globalization or glocalization?, in: **Roland Robertson/Kathleen E. White (ed.)**, Globalization: critical concepts in sociology, (London/New York: Routledge 2003), p.31

[3] **Stéphanie Paquin**, Para diplomatie et relations internationales. Théorie des stratégies internationales des régions (Bruxelles: PIE-Peter Lang, 2004)
F. Aldecoa and M. Keating, Paradiplomcy in Action. The Foreign Relations of Sub national Governments (London: Frank Cass Publisher 1999)
B. Hocking, Localizing Foreign Policy, Non-Central Governments and Multilayered Diplomacy (London: St. Martin's Press, 1993)

[4] **M. Smith and B. Hocking**, World Politics, An introduction to International Relations (Harvester: Wheatsheaf 1995) p. 175
E.H. Fry, The Expanding Role of State and Local Governments in US Foreign Affairs, (New York: Council on Foreign Relations Press 1998)

[5] see **T. Guay**, Local Government and Global Politics: The Implications of Massachusetts' "Burma Law", in: Political Science Quarterly, 115 (2000) p. 353
J. M. Kline, Continuing Controversies Over State and Local Foreign Policy Sanctions in the United States, in: Publius, 29 (2000) p. 111
Stéphanie Paquin, Les actions extérieures des entités subétatiques: quelle signification pour la politique comparée et les relations internationales? in: Revue Internationale de Politique comparée, 12/2 (2005) p. 129
Shaun Riordan, The new diplomacy, (Cambridge: Polity Press 2003), p. 81

[6] **L. Boulanger**, Les enjeux actuels de la participation du Québec à la Francophonie Multilatérale: de la paradiplomatie à la protodiplomatie, in: Politique et Société, 16/1 (1997) p. 40
Stephanie Paquin, Paradiplomatie

[7] **R.D. Putnam**, Diplomacy and Domestic Politics: the logic of two-level games, in: International Organization 42 (1988)

[8] **Christian Reus-Smit (ed.),** The politics of international law (Cambridge: Cambridge University Press 2004), p. 269,
Harold Hongju Koh, The Frankel Lecture: Bringing international law home, in: Houston Law Review, vol. 35 (1998/1999), p. 623

[9] **Paul R. Viotti/Mark V. Kauppi,** International relations theory: Realism, pluralism, globalism, (New York: Macmillan Publishing Company 1987), p. 337 (341)

Chapter 3
From national to European Foreign Service

Since the 1980's the EU has emerged as a foreign political actor in diplomacy as a consequence of the evolution of its political system and the expansion of its foreign policy-making capabilities with a strong external delegation network. This expansion of competence ran parallel to the growing economic and political weight of the EU itself. The Commission as its formal external representation became strongly involved in the conception, implementation and monitoring of development cooperation.

At present, European foreign policy is executed in three legal and political arenas: external Community policies under the EC Treaty, CFSP within the scope of the EU Treaty's second pillar and national foreign policy.[1]

By 1990 permanent external service staffs coordinating EU policy with member states interests abroad was in place which often led to an upgrading of the status of the Commission delegations. The Commission's team of international project managers had become a quasi-diplomatic service with their uniquely functional style of diplomacy (European consumer-oriented diplomatic services)[2]. Furthermore, smaller EU members not represented in third countries made special use of the services provided by the Commission delegations.[3]

The Treaty of Amsterdam in 1999 created the post of High Representative and added crisis management, conflict prevention and security issues (European Security and Defence Policy) on the EU agenda.[4]

In 2000 the European Parliament proposed the establishment of a common European Diplomacy (External Service with a College of European Diplomacy). Today, Commission delegations are accredited to 130 countries and 5 International Organizations.

In contrast to their growing number and size, their coordinating and coherence impact still remains controversial due to the strong national interests of some member states and the lack of common foreign positions especially with strategic partners. It remains to be seen whether the Commission's external relations directorates and its delegations outside the EU with their unique style of public diplomacy can form the nucleus of a new European diplomatic system such as the European External Action Service (EEAS) proposed in Article III-296 of the Draft Treaty Establishing a Constitution for Europe (2003).

Such a Europeanization[5] of an innovative diplomatic service will be dependent on the pace of future integration dynamics and will – in any event- have to face a series of fundamental legal, institutional and political issues which need consensual solutions after the rejection of the Draft Constitutional Treaty in toto by the French and Dutch electors. They basically concern the two interlinked level structures of European and member state foreign policy and their representation as well as organization within the EU.

The principal question to be addressed is the institutional and budgetary linkage of any future EEAS either to the Commission or Council Secretariat or its separation and autonomy from both (Service and budget sui generis as a new institution within the EU). This decision will then determine the composition and organization of the Service bringing together the existing Commission services and delegations, the Council services and the member states diplomats on secondment or even partly replacing national diplomatic services with integrated-international or fully joint ones. Within this context the question of duplication of staff and their terms of employment and exchange arises.

What would be the tasks of such a European Foreign Service? What kind of training would the new structures demand and who would provide it (European Diplomatic Academy)? What character and identity and political culture would it develop (Diplomatic Code of Conduct)?[6] What shape would future relations between the European Foreign Service and national diplomatic services take (substitution, subsidiarity or parallelism?)? How do they share or rationalize representational roles?

Already, the European Union plays a more proactive role in foreign policy to serve European interests and to promote common values such as democracy, sustainable development, free trade and human rights. But, only if the political will[7] (commonality of interests and values) for a strong EU foreign policy and the integration momentum is being rediscovered and strengthened, institutional and fundamental reforms of EU external relations roles can be envisaged in the future. It seems doubtful that any single Presidency can muster the necessary integrative will and popular support among its partners for this issue before the next European Elections in June 2009. But this does not exclude the option of coordinated training programmes among some European partners for their young diplomats (for example from France, Poland and Germany) as a first step.

Finally, the continuous resurgence of international crises in which the European Union becomes increasingly involved underlines the practical need to develop an institutional framework for a better coordinated and (in the interest of the population) more efficient European foreign policy by installing an EU-Foreign Minister ("single voice") at the helm of a European Foreign Service.

References

1 **Daniel Thym,** The institutional matrix of European Foreign Policy under the Constitutional Treaty, Walter-Hallstein-Institut (Humboldt-Universität zu Berlin) – Paper 05/2005, p. 16

2 **Michael Bruter,** Diplomacy without a state: the external delegations of the European Commission, in: Journal of European Public Policy, vol. 6 no. 2, 1999, p. 183

3 **Melanie Morisse-Schilbach,** Diplomatie und europäische Außenpolitik. Europäisierungseffekte im Kontext von Intergouvernementalismus am Beispiel von Frankreich und Großbritannien, (Baden-Baden: Nomos Verlag 2006), p. 182

4 **Brian Hocking / David Spence,** Towards a European Diplomatic Service? (Discussion papers in diplomacy), (Netherlands Institute of International Relations "Clingendael" 2005)
Brian Hocking / David Spence, Foreign Ministries in the European Union: Integrating Diplomats (Studies in Diplomacy), (Houndsmills, Palgrave Macmillan 2005)

5 **Alan K. Henrikson,** The future of diplomacy? Five projective visions, (Favorita Paper), in: 250 Years. Von der Orientalischen zur Diplomatischen Akademie in Wien. Symposium: A changing Europe in a changing world (Diplomatic Academy of Vienna 2006)
Andreas Maurer / Sarah Reichel, Der Europäische Auswärtige Dienst. Elemente eines Drei-Phasen-Plans, Stiftung Wissenschaft und Politik-Aktuell 53, (Berlin: Stiftung Wissenschaft und Politik November 2004)

6 **Jozef Batora,** Does the European Union transform the institution of diplomacy?, in: ARENA Workings, WP 03/6 2003, www.arena.uio.no

7 **Simon Duke,** Outcome before dogma: restarting the External Action Service debate?, in: CFSP Forum vol. 4 no.5, p.1, www.fornet.info
Stephan Keukeleire, EU Foreign Policy and (the lack of) "Political Will", in: CFSP Forum vol.4 no.5 p. 11, www.fornet.info
Jeannette Ladzik, A European diplomatic service?, in: European Policy Brief issue 20, Jan. 2006, www.fedtrust.co.uk
Melanie Morisse-Schilbach, Diplomatie und europäische Außenpolitik. p.180

Chapter 4
Symbolism and ritual in multilateral diplomacy

Traditionally the emphasis of diplomacy lies on bilateral interaction of states. With the emergence of international organizations, international conferences and summitry diplomacy turned its focus on multilateralism.

Conference diplomacy is an institution for the management of relations between governments or governments and international organizations.

Conference diplomacy has thrived for the following reasons:

- Increase in diplomatic initiatives by a growing number of states
- Proliferation of International Organizations requires a multilateral framework
- Progress in technology facilitates the organisation of large conferences
- Acceptance by the media and the general public due to its relative openness
- Ideal international stage for politicians

Summitry is conference diplomacy at the highest possible level between heads of governments/states or political leaders/highest representatives of International Organizations.[1]

While bilateralism always survived as a daily practical mode of diplomacy, with the perception of limited substantive success of large multilateral events in the past the confidentiality and closeness of bilateral diplomacy seems to be regaining new ground in globalized affairs.

Both modes of diplomacy are characterised by negotiation as a process of joint decision making for achieving peaceful and legitimate change.

The art of negotiation[2] consists of arguing and convincing the partner(s) about common interests or – in times of stagnation of the negotiating process – about the disadvantages of differing interests by claiming or creating common values or redistributing existing values.

Especially multilateral (conference) diplomacy is characterised by a strong ritualisation based on the symbolic and repetitive nature of proceedings. Ritual is understood to be a symbolic behaviour that is socially standardised and repetitive.

The feature and impact of symbolism in this context should not be underestimated since symbolic policy through its rituals demonstrates and visualises political action regardless of and independent from any substantive results. Ritual behaviour in (foreign) policy is not a mere embellishment for political activities (rational actions) but, in fact, rituals are an integral part of politics in any political system. The symbolic is real politics, articulated in a special and – via the media – most powerful way.[3]

In our media-driven society the image of a political event (real or staged) carries its own weight and shapes the mind and the hearts of the viewers on a specific topic. Such symbolic policy (for example hand-shake, public gestures etc.) has the power of surrogate action and can even substitute politics.

In diplomatic practice symbolic policy in the context of international conferences serves the following purposes:[4]

- It purports a reality in the political world by representing, confirming or legitimising a certain state of affairs (for example sovereignty and equality of participants or the disparity of their political weight, representation of a presumably orderly world). Rituals serve both to engender a particular state of affairs, and at the same time express recognition of its reality. Text and context become identical.
- It integrates all participants on a cognitive, communicative, emotional and social level and gives them – through repetitions of these events – the impression of the continuity of the world order. It even attracts and binds representatives of the civil society. Non-governmental organizations are a basic form of popular representation in the present-day world. Their participation in international conferences and international organizations is, in a way, a guarantee of the political legitimacy of these conferences or International Organizations as well as of the NGOs themselves.
- The main aim of diplomatic negotiations is to find and secure sustainable solutions through consensus or compromise. Symbolic rituals at conferences (for example handshake) can suggest unity and solidarity regardless of genuine consensus. This could delude into the perception of an understanding whereas in reality there may only exist the ambiguity of an agreed language in an official text. Nowadays, the language of UN-resolutions – for the sake of political compromise – is more often so vague that it can hardly tape over the discordance in substance which makes the execution of such a text – due to differing interpretations by the signatories – more difficult if not sometimes impossible.

- Unresolved conflicts can be kept open through symbolic conference policy. They can be tackled on a virtual level without interference in the actual relations of power. Through the rituals of communication and negotiation the perception of interaction among the parties to the conflict can be upheld and dialogue eventually resumed.
- Crises situation can be diffused or diluted in conferences through general political appeals in public as surrogates to actions or negotiation results when the political will to solve underlying problems is lacking.

The means of symbolic conference policies are a visualisation and thereby simplification of complex political problems as well as possible solutions and their consequences through rituals.[5] They generate acceptance, credibility, legitimacy and public support. The symbolic images of virtual diplomacy create political messages as claims to political power. Because of the immense power generated through political symbolism governments should proactively fill this form of representation with corresponding democratic contents, values and ideas before other forces in society monopolize and possibly misuse the power of political symbolism.

The usefulness and sustainable success of international (including UN) conferences or summit meetings will always remain a matter of considerable debate and dispute. It has proved difficult for the quality of summitry to keep in step with their quantity. They are very often criticized for their lack of effectiveness which creates a need for justification. This justification can partially be reached by a symbolisation of the impossible but necessary. The danger of international public appeasement policy through these international conferences is obvious, but it does not generally deny the possibility and future of effective multilateralism provided that it comes up with the "deliverables" of common action. Environmental diplomacy exemplifies this complexity of multilateral diplomacy.

In diplomatic practice, nevertheless, these conferences provide an ideal platform for the exchange of information and testing of ideas and to raise public awareness for global issues.[6] Presidents, heads of states and ministers need and live of such frequent and continuous dialogues with their counterparts which these fora provide. Initiatives and decisions increasingly originate in the narrow, globetrotting circles of summit-meetings (ministers or heads of state surrounded by their narrow group of personal advisors). They are the result of growing respect among statesmen. This respect is based on recognition of personal achievements of a political partner and often leads to trustworthiness in confidential consultations. The personal and confidential atmosphere of their (frequent) meetings engenders a level of credibility leading to common diplomatic positions and actions. It is a well documented fact in diplomacy that a common (mother) tongue also creates a special closeness in the relationship among statesmen. At the highest level of state representation personal trust and confidence among the leaders becomes an essential value and are to be understood as cardinal features in international politics.

References

[1] **Jan Melissen**, Summit Diplomacy Coming of Age, Discussion Papers in Diplomacy, Netherlands Institute of International Relations "Clingendael", ISSN 1569-2981, 2003

David H. Dunn, Diplomacy at the Highest Level. The Evolution of Summit Diplomacy (New York: St' Martin's Press 1996)

[2] **Thomas Risse**, "Let's Argue", p. 1 (see page 26)

[3] **Raymond Cohen**, Negotiating Across Cultures. International Communication in an Interdependent World (Washington, D.C.: United Institute of Peace Press 2002) 3rd revised edition

[4] **Raymond Cohen,** Negotiating Across Cultures, p. 216

[5] **David J. Kertzer**, Ritual, Politics, and Power, (New Haven: Yale University Press 1988)

Felicia Hughes-Freeland (ed.), Ritual, Performance, Media (London/New York: Routledge 1998)

Robert Jervis, The logic of images in international relations, (Princeton: Princeton University Press 1970)

Robert Jervis, Perception and misperception in international politics, (Princeton: Princeton University Press 1976)

[6] **Reinhard Wesel**, Symbolische Politik der Vereinten Nationen. Die "Weltkonferenzen" als Rituale (Opladen: Leske /Budrich 2004)

Chapter 5
Flexibility and pragmatism as response to global challenges

The continuum of diplomacy and diplomatic practices are suitable for the management of change in globalized relations.

In multilateral diplomacy, flexibility and pragmatism coupled with the need to find responses to new global challenges have led to a multitude of new instruments of global governance. At an operational level peace-keeping, peace-making and peace-enforcement missions with (UN-) authorized multinational forces have developed. On a military level coalitions of the willing have been forged. On a purely political level new form of consultations and contact groups among governments are continuously emerging.

These alterations in diplomatic practices do not constitute a fundamentally new diplomacy, but are instead adaptations of diplomacy to modern conditions.

I. Track-two diplomacy

One of these widely practised innovative forms of diplomacy is called track-two-diplomacy.[1] It consists of informal and unofficial interaction between influential private citizens or groups of people within a country or from different countries who are outside the formal government power structure (people-to-people diplomacy) with the goal of developing strategies to influence public opinion and to help resolve an inter- or intra-state conflict. Track-two-diplomacy therefore is an adjunct (not a substitute) to track-one-diplomacy: the conduct of negotiations between sovereign states through the medium of officials. A combination of both (double/multi-track diplomacy) at times is helpful and advisable.

Soft-track-two diplomacy intends to enhance the exchange of information and ideas for a mutual better understanding among the conflicting parties whereas hard-track-two diplomacy aims at a policy related problem solving dialogue.

Participants in the process of track-two diplomacy are non-state actors such as intellectuals, media or NGO-representatives, former civil or military servants.

As private citizens they should command a certain expertise in the conflict and be recognised by both sides as representatives of a political, economic or intellectual elite. From these unofficial representatives of their societies joint creative thinking for innovative solutions is expected. For financial or logistical support of this process third parties or sponsors such as neutral states or NGO's can be included. Their informal meetings or problem solving workshops should embrace open but confidential, exploratory, analytical, non-hierarchical and flexible discussions not bound or coerced by predetermined results. Intended to supplement official negotiations (track-one) they should give the process new vitality and impetus by

- enriching the learning process among the parties
- enhancing their flexibility
- exploring new formulas
- testing each others sincerity
- building confidence and credibility and
- breaking deadlocks

Ideally, they produce a joint concept paper with a range of policy options which will find its way into official negotiations creating new openings for binding and stabilising solutions.

Thus, track-two diplomacy is an important modern tool in international as well as national-ethnic conflicts with its impact on the participants, their governments and, last but not least, on the public through their perception and general acceptance of the diplomatic process.

II. Disaster diplomacy

Functional diplomacy is moving into the realm of theme-related or thematized diplomacy. This thematic diplomacy is contingent upon events and tends to be emergency-focussed.

Disaster tends to shatter existing norms and practices among states, creating a passing opportunity for the recognition of the fragility of life and of the common humanity bonding all peoples.[2] The concept of disaster diplomacy is based upon identifying the common interests of states at a level of shared risk and scientific knowledge. Shared risk affects all nations in a risk-prone region, whether or not they have contributed to the conditions producing the threat. Shared risk invokes public mitigation, response, and recovery. It leads to shared responsibility among all states exposed to a threat. The kind and mode of cooperation that is fostered among states affected by an environmental threat create the opportunity for change in relations among states previously in conflict. The challenge is to use that opportunity to guide actions at the micro level of disaster management so that they will lead to substantive change at the macro level of greater cooperation among states previously in conflict. Creative diplomacy for disaster reduction seems most effective at the edge of chaos in a region where there is sufficient structure to exchange information, but sufficient flexibility to adopt new alternatives to meet urgent needs.

Most recently, the tsunami which struck Indonesia, Thailand, Sri Lanka, India, the Maldives, Kenya and Somalia on 26th December 2004 has shown that natural disasters create political and diplomatic challenges as well as opportunities for disaster relief diplomacy (so called tsunami-diplomacy).

Studies by scientists and major reinsurance companies give reason to fear that both the incidents of such disasters or extreme weather events and the damage they cause will further increase in the future.

Extreme natural events are the product of a linkage between natural hazards and the vulnerability of existing social and ecological systems to these hazards. Some of the main anthropogenic influences are:

- extreme urbanisation in endangered areas and

the establishments of hazardous industries in risk-prone locations

- artificial straightening of river courses and destruction of natural flood planes
- deforestation and soil erosion and
- lack of awareness and dearth of knowledge of existing risks.

75 % of the world's population live in regions that are affected by natural disasters at least once a year. An integrated, interdisciplinary, multisectorial approach is therefore needed to address vulnerability, risk assessment and disaster management, including prevention, mitigation, preparedness, response and recovery.[3] The urgency of humanitarian action goes beyond the principal of regional equity. The disaster-related cooperation and ad hoc disaster support in complex humanitarian emergencies (affecting more than one state, involving a proliferation of the number and types of actors) can have catalytic spill-over effects leading to sustained and improved relations between states with deep-rooted animosities or in zones of heightened antagonism or internal conflict and can open doors to effective peace making diplomacy.

The principal point is that disasters provide diplomatic opportunities, but those opportunities are not necessarily grasped because reasons other than disaster-related activities influence diplomatic activities. Disaster-related activities can impact and catalyze diplomatic activities in a manner chosen by the different actors. Its actors choose that catalysis can be made to happen and disaster diplomacy can be put into action.[4] Disaster-related activities can be opportunities to demonstrate that cooperation can provide dividends. The long-term results from targeted, shorter-term confidence-building activities can be important in globalized affairs.

The exploitation of critical happenings can set a nation and a region on a long forward course. Disasters, thus, may have a multiplying and legitimising effect on diplomatic rapprochement upon recognition of mutual interests by the parties.

The common management of disaster risks in the form of tsunami-diplomacy increasingly yields not only a humanitarian imperative but also, more importantly, a strategic component of regional security, economic cooperation and sustainable development. States recognise that cooperation (and not only competition) is imperative for the mutual benefit in the future. The impact is to be seen rather in terms of the development, and not the initiation, of ties between governments. Disaster relief thus opens a new dimension and justification for modern diplomacy. Thematized diplomacy creates a challenge for traditional diplomacy in order to strive to maintain, on the basis of well-situated facilities a constancy of presence and continuity of representation. Their capacity to react results from their constant presence. Temporary task forces and special missions consisting of outsiders and experts cannot replace the local knowledge or sensitivity and indeed accountability of the diplomatic representation and their coordinating efforts.

The motivations for disaster relief diplomacy can be characterised by one or a combination of the following factors:

- humanitarian considerations
- political expediency (or enlightened self-interest) or
- legal obligation.[5]

Humanitarian considerations have first been legally sanctioned by the International Court of Justice in the Corfu Channel case condemning the failure of the Albanian authorities to warn British warships of the danger to which they were exposed by the mine-field in the Albanian territorial waters:

> "Such obligations are based, not only on the Hague Convention of 1907 no. VIII which is applicable in time of war, but on certain general and well recognised principles, namely elementary considerations of humanity, even more exacting in peace than in war."[6]

The connection between economic development and political stability in solving international problems is also enunciated in article 1 (3) of the UN-Charter which mentions international cooperation of an economic, social, cultural or humanitarian character.

A new international mind-set including a change of attitude at governmental level in accordance with the complex size of such disaster and the shortened reaction time is needed to build up the necessary preventive and ad hoc structures for relief. The existing tools of cooperative diplomacy have to be adapted to these new challenges.

The factor of political expediency (or enlightened self-interest) can be closely linked to the international agenda of the preservation of the common heritage of mankind (global commons), especially from ecological disaster.

The question of a legal obligation for the international community to provide humanitarian disaster relief is a matter for controversy since any unilateral intervention also would affect the principle of state sovereignty. The perception of a legal obligation to provide disaster relief has tentatively been based on articles 22 and 25 of the Universal Declaration of Human Rights and articles 2, 7 and 11 of the International Covenant on Economic, Social and Cultural Rights. But this political claim[7] – not yet endorsed by international practice – can only be placed – de lege ferenda – on the agenda of an emerging international law.

There are yet no internationally agreed standards for donor and beneficiary government action in the form of a body of international disaster repsonse law as customary law.[8] Here, the principle of solidarity (of a State with the population in another state affected by natural disaster) embedded in international law through resolutions of the UN General Assembly could develop from a moral to a legal obligation to render assistance.[9]

References

1 **Karin Aggestam**, Two-Track Diplomacy: Negotiations between Israel and the PLO through open and secret channels, in: **Jönsson/Langhorne**, Diplomacy, vol. III Nr. 51
Shai Feldman (ed.), Track-II Diplomacy. Lessons from the Middle East, (Cambridge, Massachusetts: MIT Press 2001)
Alain Gresh / Dominique Vidal, Les 100 clés du Proche-Orient, (Paris: Hachette 1996)
Dalia Dassa Kaye, Track two diplomacy and regional security in the Middle East, in: International Negotiation 2001 (6:1), p. 49
Daniel Lieberfeld, Evaluating the contributions of track two diplomacy to conflict termination in South Africa, in: Journal of Peace Research 2002 (39:3), p. 355
John W. McDonald, Further exploration of Track Two Diplomacy, in: **Louis Kriesberg / Stuart J Thorson (ed.)**, Timing the de-escalation in international conflicts (Syracuse, NY: Syracuse University Press 1991) p. 201
Louise Diamond / John McDonald, Multi-track Diplomacy: A Systems Approach to Peace, (West Hartford: Kumarian Press 1996)
Joseph V. Montville, Transnationalism and the Role of Two Track Diplomacy, in: S. **Thompson / K. Jensen / R. Smith / K. Schraub (ed.)**, Approaches to Peace: an Intel-

lectual Map (Washington: United States Institute of Peace Press 1991)
Joseph V. Montville, The arrow and the olive branch: A case for Track Two Diplomacy, in: **John W. McDonald/Diane B. Bendahmane (ed.)**, Conflict Resolution: Track Two Diplomacy, (Washington: Institute for Multi-Track Diplomacy 1995), p. 9
Nadim N. Rouhana, Unofficial Intervention: Potential Contributions to Resolving Ethno-National Conflicts, in: **Jan Melissen**, Innovation in Diplomatic Practice

2 **Louise K. Comfort,** Disaster: Agent of diplomacy or change in international affairs?, in: Cambridge Review of International Affairs vol. 14 (2000) No. 1, p. 277

3 Report of the World Summit on Sustainable Development in Johannesburg in 2002, Annex, Plan of Implementation of the World Summit on Sustainable Development (Document A / Conf.199/20)

4 **Ilan Kelman**, Acting on disaster diplomacy, in: Journal of International Affairs, Spring/Summer 2006, vol. 59 No.2, p.215

5 **Boniface Okere/Ernest M. Makawa**, Global Solidarity and the International Response to Disasters, in: **David D. Caron / Charles Leben (ed.)**, The International Aspects of Natural and Industrial Catastrophes, (The Hague: Hague Academy of International Law 2001) p. 429
Ilan Kelman / Theo Konkis, Disaster Diplomacy: Discord Disintegrated, in: Cambridge Review of International Affairs, 2000 Vol. XIV No. 1, p. 214
Dimitris Keridis, Earthquakes, diplomacy, and new thinking in foreign policy, in: The Fletcher Forum of World Affairs, vol. 30:1 (Winter 2006), p. 207

6 ICJ Reports 1949 22

7 **J.W. Samuels**, Organised Responses to Natural Disaster, in: **Mac Donald, Johnson and Morris (eds.)**, The International Law and Policy of Human Welfare, (Alphen aan den Rijn: Sijthoff & Noordhoff 1978)

8 **Michael H. Hoffmann,** What is the scope of international disaster response law?, in: International disaster response laws, principles and practice: reflections, prospects and challenges (IDRL) (Geneva: International Federation of Red Cross and Red Crescent Societies 2004), p. 13

9 **Rüdiger Wolfrum,** Solidarity amongst States: An emerging structural principle of International Law, in: **Pierre-Marie Dupuy/Bardo Fassbender/Malcolm N. Shaw/ Karl-Peter Sommermann(ed.),** Common values in International Law. Essays in honour of Christian Tomuschat, (Kehl: N.P. Engel Verlag 2006) p. 1087 (1098)

Chapter 6
Reciprocity versus communitarianism

Reciprocity is a guiding principle in domestic as well as international law,[1] but it is also a normative theme and practice in international relations.[2] It has been called the soul, machinery or driving force of diplomacy.[3]

Generally accepted in domestic legal systems by specific norms and institutions it also dominates the international legal order in lack of a centralised enforcement system. Reciprocity serves as a rational for international treaties as well as the emergence of customary law. The constructive force and stabilizing function of reciprocity as a legal principle rely on the sovereign equality of states and the contractual quid pro quo (mutual advantage, give and take, rights and obligations) of their interactions. Reciprocity can be considered a meta-rule for the system of international law, but it is not a panacea to resolve all issues in international law.[4]

Apart from serving as the basis for any legal structure in society (suum cuisque tribuere) reciprocity is also invoked as an appropriate standard of behaviour which can produce cooperation among sovereign states. According to this diplomatic concept and practice a sovereign state will grant rights and advantages to another state to the extent that it will receive similar goods or services in return. In social interchange, reciprocal obligations of contingency (on rewarding reactions) and rough equivalence (of benefits) hold societies together.

In diplomatic practice, two basic forms of reciprocity can be distinguished: Specific and diffuse reciprocity. While the concept of specific reciprocity leads to simultaneous exchange or one with strictly delimited sequence (simultaneity), diffuse reciprocity provides mutual benefits sequentially or over a long term (sequentiality). A combination of both is not unusual in globalized (trade) relations.

For practical purposes, another distinction concerning the concept of reciprocity can be made according to its effect of commutative justice and that of distributive justice. The first is based on the satisfaction of mutual self-interests, the latter reaches beyond into the realm of global public interest enhancing social solidarity and community interests where public goods are concerned.

A globalized society emerges when the participants are conscious of certain common interests and common values and act to preserve the "global commons" or common concerns of humankind. These fundamental moral values and responsibilities intend to reconcile individualism with universalism in order to face the common challenges of today and tomorrow. These value of the "public weal" are not the sum of the states particular interests but form today's common heritage of mankind: Democratic practises, human rights, social, political, economic development, protection of the environment, survival of mankind.

The rise of transnational human rights networks and social movements can be regarded as first signs of new collective identities and ethics beyond the state. The debate about transnational democracy and the increasing commitment to improve the living conditions of people of other nationalities and ethnicities indicate something like a world society.

The present problems that are endangering these public goods (in the shape of public bads) are:

- Disasters and epidemics
- International crime/terrorism
- illegal migration / trafficking in persons
- Cultural, religious and ethnic extremism.

As a matter of survival we need to deliver comprehensive responses to these challenges facing us all by exploring common avenues. Diplomacy can play a crucial role in the process of promoting and producing these values on a global level.

Since reciprocal/mutual concessions are difficult to materialize in positional conference bargaining multilateral diplomacy is governed by the concept of communitarianism substituting any formal or substantial, specific or diffuse reciprocity with the aim of global good governance,[5] which is driven by public interest and social solidarity.[6]

Since modern parts of international law are being based upon common interests and values of the international community requiring common action and reflecting the transformation of international law into a value based international legal order solidarity in the form of communitarianism can be considered an emerging structural principle in international law.[7]

The concept of good governance emerged in the 1980s in the international financial and development organizations. The concept's premise is that of a democratic state based on the rule of law, with political legitimating and a state monopoly on the use of violence. Its institutions act on the basis of human rights principles – non-discrimination and equal opportunities, transparency, accountability, participation and empowerment of the people. Good governance – on a national level – basically means a responsible approach to political power and public resources to ensure sustainable development benefiting all sections of the population.

An interesting question is whether the legal status of the components of good governance (popular participation in decision-making, and its control through transparency and mechanisms of accountability) has turned good governance into a norm of customary international law.[8]

- Outside specific human rights treaties accountability cannot be considered a legally binding element of good governance. One might consider Article 25 lit. a of the International Covenant on Civil and Political Rights as a duty under international law to ensure public participation in state activities (participatory governance), but such an obligation to permit public participation in the decision-making process has not been recognized by the Human Rights Committee and would – in any case – only be binding for the parties to the Covenant.
- In a regional context, the legal obligations to democratic governance formulated for the Council of Europe and in the Inter-American Democratic Charter do not oblige states to transfer decision-making powers to civil society.
- With regard to transparency, a customary right to transparency cannot be drawn from the freedom of expression as a purely protective principle.

But, on the basis of repeated confirmation of the concept of good governance by UN member states in international declarations and the growing common standard of achievement good governance may be considered as an emerging legal principle of customary international law.

In the international debate on development today, the lack of good governance is regarded as one of the prime causes of failing states, human rights deficits and poverty.

Trans- and international cooperation is required to meet governance challenges and these governance challenges are placed on the public agenda. In the pursuit of communitarianism or the public weal as a transnational concept a new world order of global good governance could emerge. While the traditional form of reciprocity is declining, communitarianism is rising as a major concern in globalized relations. In the 21st century communitarianism replaces the struggle for the balance of power and the strife for peaceful coexistence as an international leitmotiv and competes with traditional self-interest in our globalized world. Power-oriented diplomacy develops into rule-oriented diplomacy.

Community interests and the upgrading of common interests emerge as the antitheses to bilateralism. They are perceived as a consensus that certain fundamental values are not to be left to the free disposition of states individually or inter se but they are to be seen as a matter of concern to all states permeating into a socially conscious legal order with appropriate social responsibility and accountability. This promotes the concept of global commons and communalizes international relations beyond traditional governmental interaction. The universalisation of such basic values and their implementation in a global community is expressed in the UN Charter and its conventions on human rights. These community elements are nowadays overlapping, superseding and sometimes even abolishing the old-fashioned bilateralism structures in order to embody a common interest of all states and, indirectly, of mankind. This representation and priorization of common interests counterbalances the egoistic interests of states.[9]

The tendency towards international and supranational organizations and their enlargement (such as the European Union) underlines the growing attraction of the principle of communitarianism.

Yet, this tendency is not undisputed in practice. The dispute reflects the opposing perspectives of progressive regime-change on one side and regime-persistence in support of the status quo on the other side. With an expanding communitarianism some states could fear an increasing loss of their sovereignty. But, the growing number of participants in modern diplomacy is already accompanied by a redefinition of sovereignty due to the tendency away from governance by government via governance with government (cooperation of governments with networks of other public and private actors) to the perspective of governance without government (self-regulation and self-coordination by non-state actors or civil society) which are transforming and to some extent undermining statehood.

The rise of communitarianism is therefore to be seen as an integral part of the ongoing transformation of globalized relations and its impact on diplomacy. It gradually changes the finality of international interaction.

In international law, the concept of erga omnes obligations (with reference to community interests)[10] can already be considered as a result of this development.

References

1 **Bruno Simma**, Reciprocity, in: Encyclopaedia of Public International Law, (Amsterdam: Elsevier 2000), vol. 4, p. 29
Emmanuel Decaux, La réciprocité en droit international, (Paris: Bibliothèque de droit international 1980)

2 **Robert O. Keohane**, Reciprocity in international relations, in: International Organization, 40/1, Winter 1986, p.1
D.W.Larson, Exchange and reciprocity, in: International Negotiations 1998, p. 121
R. J. Leng, Reciprocity in recurring crises, in: International Negotiations 1998, p. 197
Geoff R. Berridge, Reciprocity, in: **G.R. Berridge (with Alan James**) A Dictionary of Diplomacy

3 For the history see: **Geoff R. Berridge**, in: **Christer Jonsson/Martin Hall,** Essence of Diplomacy, p. 50

4 **Francesco Parisi/Nita Ghei,** The role of reciprocity in international law, in: Cornell International Law Journal vol. 36 (2003) p. 93

5 **James N. Rosenau**, Governance and democracy in a globalizing world, in: **Daniele Archibugi/David Held/Martin Köhler (ed.**), Re-imagining political community. Studies in cosmopolitan democracy, (Cambridge: Cambridge University Press 1998) p. 28
James N. Rosenau / Ernst-Otto Czempiel (ed.), Governance without Government: Order and Challenge in World Politics, (Cambridge: Cambridge University Press 1992)

6 In French sociology the term "solidarité hiérarchique" is used by **Guillaume Devin**, Sociologie des relations internationales, p.97
Guillaume Devin, La loyauté: d'un monde à l'autre, in: **Josepha Laroche**, La loyauté dans les relations internationales, (Paris: L'Harmattan 2001) p. 371

7 **Rüdiger Wolfrum,** Solidarity amongst States: An Emerging Structural Principle of International Law, in: **Pierre-Marie Dupuy/Bardo Fassbender/Malcolm N. Shaw/ Karl-Peter Sommermann (ed.),** Common Values in International Law. Essays in Honour of Christian Tomuschat, (Kehl: N.P. Engel Verlag 2006), p. 1087

8 **Beate Rudolf**, Is "Good Governance" a norm in international law?, in: **Pierre-Marie Dupuy/Bardo Fassbender/Malcolm N. Shaw/Karl-Peter Sommermann (ed.**), Common values in international law, p. 1007

9 **Bruno Simma**, From bilateralism to community interest in international law, in: Recueil des cours de l'Académie de droit international de La Haye, Tome 250, vol.VI (1994), p. 229

10 **Maurizio Ragazzi,** The concept of international obligations erga omnes (Oxford: Clarendon Press 2000), p. 218

Part II
Transformation of globalized relations and its impact on diplomacy

Chapter 7
New participants and corporate diplomacy: symbiosis of diplomacy and transnational companies

In April 2004, the UN Security Council in New York examined possible ways of avoiding future international conflicts. On that occasion, a leading representative of the German business community spoke for the first time to the Security Council: Dr. Heinrich von Pierer, the current Chairman of the Supervisory Board of the Siemens Group. Before the supreme UN body, where government representatives and diplomats normally speak, he stated:

> "Business alone cannot change the world but, together with public partners, business can make decisive contributions in the struggle against violence, against anarchy and against terrorism, and on behalf of civilization, freedom and prosperity."

Josef Ackermann, Spokesman of the Board of Managing Directors of Deutsche Bank, was quoted as saying at the Annual Colloquium of the Alfred Herrhausen Society in Berlin that environmental disasters, epidemics and financial crises had meant that the nation-state had reached its limits. New forms of cooperation were needed (with civil society) which he called "temporary partnerships of responsibility".

These leading businessmen personify the international manager at the intersection between transnational business, politics and diplomacy. Von Pierer's address to the UN Security Council can certainly be regarded as the high point to date in the development of a global civil society[1] which has been ever more visible since the end of the Cold War but whose contours were already apparent before then. As far back as the 1930s, the German constitutional and international law expert Heinrich Triepel outlined a "foreign policy of private individuals" which today includes NGOs and multinational companies:

> "It is the responsibility of the government to conduct foreign policy. And in fact, as a rule, it is the state and the state alone that submits itself to this task. The foreign policy of private individuals often exerts a sig-

> nificant influence on the political and legal relations between their state and other states."[2]

The opening up of national markets and the IT revolution brought about by the Internet have resulted in traditional state tasks increasingly being assumed by private players who no longer have to stop at national borders when it comes to using resources. They can shift them almost unhindered to those locations which offer them the most favourable conditions. For example, one third of international transactions already take place within transnational companies.

The budgets of some of them are larger than those of some nation-states. They offer enormous resources in innovation and thought, leadership, advocacy, popular mobilization, financial investment and service delivery in the pursuit of some global public goods such as health, education, security, and environmental protection.

With the rising expectations of governmental services on the part of the populations and the inability of states to perform, individuals and communities are beginning to look elsewhere to fill these needs. Nowadays, many transnational corporations are providing needed goods and services to groups that states formerly provided, thus creating a parallel authority alongside governments.

The resulting asymmetry between economic areas and state regulatory levels leads to competition among states which lends transnational companies a new position of power and gives rise to new opportunities and responsibilities for actively influencing and shaping global policy. This development can also entail a shift of power on the part of governments.[3]

At the same time, new private interest groups with social rather than economic objectives are emerging. These NGOs are a manifestation of a new information society in which the state no longer has a monopoly on inexpensive sources of news. Rather, the gathering of information lies in the hands of global media networks which individual states find difficult to control due to their transnational character. These, too, are evidence of a new civil society. The new technologies have made possible international networking independent of state information services and an unprecedented collation of knowledge. In many areas, acknowledged experts are no longer to be found in state agencies but in private think tanks and operational teams which frequently have a larger budget than the corresponding governmental organization. It is therefore no longer possible to imagine today's world of politics without them acting as advisors. At the same time, NGOs can use this knowhow effectively in conjunction with the new media in order – also beyond state borders – to influence public opinion. They have thus become a force with direct influence which can contribute to the democratic system of checks and balances.

The NGOs as part of the international civil society can deploy their populist and indirect rule towards the privatization of public authority and responsibility and become a partial surrogate of the state.[4]

In view of their transnational nature and their accelerating complexity, as well as the increasing brevity of international development stages, current problems, for example environmental protection, development assistance, disaster reduction and management, and fighting crime, can only be resolved in cooperation with non-state participants.

These developments mean that the traditional definition of diplomacy as the "cultivation of relations between sovereign states (and international organizations) by accredited representatives", which dates back to the Peace of Westphalia, has to be supplemented as follows today: "cultivation of relations between sovereign states (and international organizations) including other international players".[5] The trend towards globalization and transnational economic relations[6] thus also forces diplomacy to radically reorientate itself towards complementarity and a cooperative culture in the changing international network of relations. Transnational relations are defined as regular interactions across national boundaries when at least one participant is a non-state agent or does not operate on behalf of a national government or an intergovernmental organization. It is becoming increasingly clear that diplomacy has acquired a new task, the management of change, along-side its traditional function, the management of order.[7]

Diplomacy's dealings nowadays with new non-state participants demand a continual readiness to engage in dialogue between state (as sovereignty-bound actor) and non-state partners (as sovereignty-free actors). They all form part of an extended diplomatic dialogue. In order to function in this new political environment, these participants must be flexible and less dependent on traditional structures and established routines.

Civil society organizations can play a very important and constructive role in supporting the state. They complement rather than replace the work of politicians.[8] Therefore, this is about the qualitative change in traditional forms of multilateral cooperation within the framework of international regimes and the trend towards global political networks.

The role of transnational groups within the network of international politics, which is increasingly interlinked and transcends borders, also has to be redefined. Some observers fear that as a result of the power shift from the political influence of nation-state participants to private-sector entities, the "primacy of politics" will be superseded by the "primacy of economics". It is right to say that although the economization of foreign policy restricts (external) national sovereignty, it creates new partnerships of responsibility among politics, industry and society[9] which are in the interests of everyone concerned.

Transnational companies act as participants in the international context (corporate diplomacy) at three levels:

- They try through statements, talks or publicity campaigns to influence the national decisionmaking process in the field of foreign policy.
- They establish direct contacts with foreign governments in order to put forward their interests.
- They exert political influence through contacts with international organizations.
- They lobby within corporate diplomacy.

"Diplomatic advisers" or "corporate diplomats" should therefore be positioned within the organization and hierarchy of the management of international companies in a way that allows them to use their experience to ensure that foreign policy and diplomatic customs are given due consideration in operative business practices.[10] Some of them are already positioned in "External Affairs and Public Policy Sections" at the top of the management with the task of "geopolitical engineering".

The prerequisites for this position are the skills of a "traditional" diplomat, such as an outlook and mentality shaped by foreign policy, expertise which can be used on the international stage, mastery of the technique of bilateral and multilateral negotiations, practical knowledge of diplomatic instruments, procedures, modus operandi, communication lines, as well as protocol practices.[11] In future, these qualifications will, among other things, be the key to becoming a high-profile business manager of international standing.[12]

Furthermore, it is conceivable that in regions of the world where state infrastructure is either absent or inadequate, transnational companies could, on a temporary basis, carry out services and tasks (e.g. in the fields of food supplies, educations, health service, energy, transport, security) either through contracting out/outsourcing or with international toleration, They would thus – without either democratic legitimacy or control – assume social responsibility.

Legitimacy basically is the right to do something in society in this context, it means that institutions and the decisions they take must be seen as fair and acceptable to all relevant stakeholders if they are to be effective in changing public and private behaviour. Claims to legitimacy can be based on the following criteria[13]:

- representation
- legal bases

- competence
- moral legitimacy
- Public benefit.

The process of deinstitutionalization leads to the politicizing of society with subsequent problems of legitimacy of forms of governance beyond the nation-state. Today, legitimacy is measured in the effective problem-solving capacity (output-legitimacy) based on strong commitment to principles of equity grounded in civil society. The logic of effective problem-solving transfers into the logic of legitimate governance. The accepted problem-solving by private participants in global governance also has the potential to strengthen the modern version of participatory democracy through discursive interaction between several participants and structures.

Private participants are particularly well-qualified for the following reasons:

- Transnational companies have a global information and communications network with a web of personal relations. Staff levels in their offices abroad are often higher than those of diplomatic missions.
- Their decision-making structures are less hierarchical and thus more flexible than those of state bodies.
- They often have additional expertise and contacts on the ground which can be of help particularly in conflict situations and in the absence of state structures ("agents of access").

This is about transnational companies temporarily substituting the state and performing some of its management of order functions and providing assistance in the absence or as a complement to intact state service institutions. With regard to the fragmentation of the state's monopoly on power, the transnational companies' lack of political legitimacy can be compensated in the short term by the stabilizing effect of their authority on the ground. Other advantages of cooperative solutions are:

- Independent expertise and competence in solving problems can improve results beyond legitimate economic interests and be of benefit to foreign policy as a whole.
- Political transparency enhances the national and international acceptance of foreign policy action.
- Civil society forces can, e.g. via the media, help mobilize society in the sphere of foreign policy.
- State negotiating positions can be strengthened internationally in cooperation with NGOs and multinational companies.
- In the field of international development cooperation, this cooperation can provide greater access to the population.

- Common and durable interest in global stability.

The most significant indication so far of a growing sense of social responsibility among transnational companies ("good corporate citizenship")[14] is the Global Compact on regulating crossborder business transactions. On the initiative of UN Secretary-General Kofi Annan, some 50 chairmen of transnational companies undertook in July 2000 in collaboration with the UN to comply with the human rights, labour, social and environmental standards derived from the UN's central objectives by exercising corporate social responsibility. During the last four years, the Global Compact has developed into a multi-stakeholder network with more than 1700 members in 70 countries, including 31 with their headquarters in Germany (www.unglobalcompact.org).

The Global Compact has opened a cooperative arena for common action between new participants to solve global problems and brought along a paradigmatic change from traditional power play to a learning and dialogue process.

Due to its voluntary nature, however, the Compact does not have the same effect as a directive. Rather, its impact is felt through the resulting exchange of information. It should also be noted that the Compact can and should neither replace nor rule out political or legal measures by the international community but should instead complement them in a pragmatic and creative manner.

With regard to the legal nature of the Compact's ten basic principles it should be noted that based on voluntary selfregulation they represent neither a code of conduct nor a directive (such as, for example, the OECD Principles of Corporate Governance). From a legal point of view, the Global Compact is not a binding catalogue of regulations (under international law), nor is it "soft law". It is not binding as a minimum standard but, rather, contains flexible guidelines for best practices. These are not subject to any control or accountability, nor to sanctions. To date, companies have rejected any higher form of codification.

Corporate social responsibility is not an expression of philanthropy but an investment of private capital (sometimes in partnership of responsibility with NGOs) for social services which create social values, thus an investment in the future of humanity. It can also manage negative impacts of the company and improve its reputation as a result (image booster) with positive repercussions even for shareholders.

The German Government has supported the partnership approach of the Global Compact since the outset. It is particularly interested in the issue of the responsibility shouldered by companies in conflict scenarios and is striving for the adoption of a Security Council or General Assembly Resolution on creating a global framework for fostering business practices which takes into account those aspects which could contribute to conflicts.

Irrespective of the character of the voluntary selfregulation practised by transnational companies, a fundamental structural change of the international system, as well as of international law, are already being considered in academic circles in view of the emergence of non-state participants in a globalized world. In particular, a change in international law would involve extending the circle of subjects of international law to include private actors. However, deliberations on this are not new. For example in 1978, the International Arbitral Tribunal[15] found that an international company can be the holder of limited international legal personality.[16] In 2001 the International Court of Justice ruled that the USA not only was in breach of art. 36 para. 1 b) of the Vienna Convention on Consular Relations concerning Germany but also violated the rights of two individuals.[17] With regard to the international legal personality of individuals, the establishment of the International Criminal Tribunals[18] as well as the International Criminal Court provide the milestones clarifying that private persons are bound by international customary law.

However, in the question of a general extension of the circle of subjects of international law, the fact that there is no generally recognized definition of the term international legal personality in academic circles is problematic. As far back as 1978, limiting this circle to sovereign states, international organizations, the Holy See, as well as the Order of Malta, was no longer adequate. Some describe as international law every relationship whose partners are not subject to the jurisdictions of the other side. Others believe that the status of being a subject of international law is linked to a capability to use force. Thürer[19] summarizes this contrast under the terms "sovereignty as the highest authority" and "capability". Here, too, it remains disputed whether these have the necessary or sufficient character to act as conditions for international legal personality.

Despite this controversy, however, there are already concrete concepts on how private actors could be included in international law. For example, Wildhaber proposed a functional statehood[20] in 1978. Here private players only have international legal personality vis-à-vis their state contracting partners – that is to say, on a case-to-case basis – not, however, a generally valid status under international law.

The theory put forward by McDougall and Lasswell goes much further. They say that a policy-oriented process requires the inclusion of all parties involved in decision-making in an international law system.[21]

However, critics such as Delbrück[22] fear that recognition of international law status would mean that states lose control over private actors.

As an alternative, a supranational regulatory policy – as already in place within the framework of the control of competition in Europe – has been suggested. This "constitutional approach" means: Having access to the global level, these new actors cannot be controlled by individual states alone. They can rather easily avoid national control by going international. So the task of states, if they still want to control the activities of NGOs and multi-national enterprises, is to agree upon rules of international law enabling states to exercise control anywhere, and not only on the territory where an NGO has its seat.

NGOs are seen to be both a challenge to and a realisation of democratic representation. On one hand, there is no obligation for an NGO to operate within a democratic internal structure (though some do), on the other hand, NGOs are articulating, at the national and the international level, interests that could othewise remain unrepresented. In this respect, already former UN Secretary General Boutros Boutros-Ghali commentedon the NGOs as an indispensable part of the legitimacy of the UN.

The question of extending the circle of subjects of international law to include NGOs has not yet led to the latter being lent international law status. However, it cannot be denied that an international system of non-state participants has emerged alongside the system of states. A rethinking of the role and function of these participants will also imply changing the legal status of NGOs. In particular, the practice of international organizations of accrediting NGOs for consultations will foster the further development of international law. Of the approx. 50,000 NGOs, 4000 are registered with the UN as advisory bodies. If the increased participation of NGOs in international governance is to be effective, efficient and have a meaningful lasting effect, it requires institutional rights and duties – and with it a (functional, partial) legal personality. Thus, legal personality of non-state actors can be taken as a minimum safeguarding clause for surmounting the legitimacy deficit of international organizations.[23] In the context of legitimacy it is important to note that NGOs are widely considered to be capable of carrying the rights and accompanying obligations of international law.

A recent study of 31 International Organizations has revealed that in the majority of cases, International Organizations do confer legal personality[24] to NGOs, mostly in form of subject or person status. Moreover, they predominantly have done so from the early days of their existence. International Organizations seem to be quite sympathetic to according legal personality to NGOs – direct and indirect personality alike -, but remain rather static with regard to the status model once chosen – with a declining affinity of new organizations to introducing personal status. Altogether, this has led to an increasing breadth and density of NGO legal personality which might be capable of absorbing some of the critics with regard to the legitimacy deficit of international organizations.[25] International law cannot altogether ignore political reality, NGOs must be able to operate in the world as it is.

The German Foreign Office decided early on to cooperate with non-state participants: In the wake of globalization there are many partners pursuing a policy of internationalization. Non-governmental organizations, whether they are humanitarian aid organizations or companies, are important players in the international field. The German Government has endeavoured with its offer of dialogue to involve the various participants in a joint discussion. But state foreign policy is not a relict of the past which can take second place in the age of globalization to individual players. State foreign policy is a force which should retain an overview of the various activities and trends, which should intervene to give direction, which should coordinate.

Such steering and coordination by the state presupposes precise knowledge of the way in which non-state participants work and their decision-making structures. Only those who know the internal processes of their partners can serve their needs and make possible a successful dialogue.

The Federal Ministry of the Interior and the Federal Ministry of Finance have therefore been participating since October 2004 in an exchange programme between civil servants and employees of leading companies in the automotive, aeronautical and financial sectors and the German Foreign Office is already taking part in this programme.

The German Foreign Office already regularly accepts representatives of business associations and companies for shortterm assignments. An exchange of personnel of this kind and the ensuing cooperative culture would lead to a linking of expertise with experience and practice in the field of foreign policy and could result in a cross-fertilization of domestic and foreign policy experience and problem-solving. This symbiosis of diplomacy and multinational companies is of benefit to both sides.[26]

Companies are given an opportunity to gain an insight into diplomatic customs which are of ever greater importance to them due to their growing international power and the increasing political responsibility which this brings with it. The German Foreign Office, on the other hand, can help guarantee that state and non-state participants maintain a uniform line abroad and, at the same time, participate in the internal network of information and relations among international companies.

Diplomacy today involves an increasing number of participants who are experts in matters other than diplomacy and hold their positions outside the foreign affairs administration. This evolution marks the end of the traditional principle of diplomatic representation limited to states and their agents. With the emergence of globalized networks of authorities and entities new participants beyond the state appear on the diplomatic stage. They develop their own representational mechanisms to manage the complex relationship in the globalized relations.

The operational requirements of transnational companies and NGOs on a global basis resemble those of diplomatic services. In their intercorporate relations, mergers or takeovers as well as dealings with foreign governments they need the same negotiating and mediating skills and structures as in traditional diplomatic negotiations. They face the same problems of cross-cultural negotiations and need the similar strategies to overcome them. For their political risk assessments and decisions they are also involved in the internal developments of the country they operate in trying to influence policies in favour of their interests.

As transnational companies deepen their engagement with governments, international institutions and nongovernmental organizations they need new, diplomatic capacities, skill-sets, soft powers and capabilities as well as intangible assets such as relationships, expertise and reputation for effective communication, negotiation and representation. In the face of necessity they appoint their own representatives with changing forms of representation for example in the case of transnational companies to organizations and communities outside their traditional stakeholders. As they enter and influence the new world of diplomacy their competence and confidence in diplomacy will grow while adapting to its norms and principles.

Diplomatic practices can offer a set of best practices which can be used by the new participants to guide and optimize their actions in globalized relations. This is especially relevant in their contacts with governmental authorities. Transnational companies are increasingly becoming conscious of how much they can learn from governments. International business managers today must take a world view and recognise the political role that their companies increasingly have with their host governments. As they learn to use nation-building techniques in order to gain popular legitimacy, businessmen move into areas of activity which, as yet, they barely comprehend, but which are very familiar to politicians and diplomats. They are carrying out their own informal-political diplomacy, more often without intimate knowledge of the style and subtlety of diplomatic discourse, and therefore need a staff of corporate diplomats to combine local expertise and broad experience of dealing with governments in other countries. This includes personal rapport and intimate knowledge of the strings of power by the politicians, officials as well as the opposition to search and cultivate common grounds and mutual interest. Corporate diplomacy can provide training in negotiating techniques with foreign governments and civil societies as well as in political, cultural and social differences in order to better position the transnational companies in the international environment. This learning process could also help provide an early warning system of potential developments and prevent frictions and crises.

Far from being a oneway street, diplomacy on the other hand can profit from transnational business methods and management experiences. The penetration of marketing techniques into the public diplomacy of governments indicates the profound adaptation and reformation which the professional diplomacy is undergoing. In response to this modernization challenge the diplomatic profession should adopt some of the same privatesector methods, including branding and marketing.

This mutual impregnation of diplomacy and business can best be organized in joint training programs at all levels, including diplomatic as well as international managerial skills. Ideally, they should be enriched by interdisciplinary research results from academics with appropriate international exposure. These elements jointly form the core of Corporate Diplomacy creating a common language and behaviour in globalized relations. Even before government or business the academic world in the United States of America, Australia and the Netherlands has recognized this need and opportunity: The Karl F. Landegger Program in International Business Diplomacy of the Edmund A. Walsh School of Foreign Service at Georgetown University offers such postgraduate courses for corporate diplomats of the future. The primary mission of the Landegger Program is to train students for work at the intersection of international public and private sector activities. The multidisciplinary course (including theory and practice of international negotiations and international risk analysis) is intended to bridge the differences in perception and communication that often separate these vital segments of society.

In a similar vain the Asia-Pacific College of Diplomacy at the Australian National University provides a Master of Diplomacy Compulsory Course on transnational diplomacy which pays particular attention to developments of crossborder partnerships between state and non-state actors in setting and promoting multilateral political agendas. Annual Transnational Policy Forum activities are giving students the opportunity to interact with diplomatic practitioners and learn through firsthand experience. Students completing a Master of Diplomacy with prior diplomatic experience in an embassy may be seeking advancement within their department or perhaps senior management employment with a corporation with an international orientation.

The Clingendael Diplomatic Studies Programme organizes at the Netherlands Institute of International Relations "Clingendael" in The Hague four day seminars on multilateral and cross-cultural negotiations for diplomats, other senior civil servants and representatives of international corporations. The programme is offering both theory and practice of multilateral negotiation in international organizations and companies in the fields of politics, economics, trade, energy, environment and security. Through case studies and roleplays the process of preparation, procedures, skills, strategies and techniques and their evaluation is trained. Negotiation styles and strategies are discussed, and attention is paid to cross-cultural negotiation and the influence of cultural factors. Moreover, the behaviour of successful negotiators is analysed.

A survey conducted with the support of the German Foreign Office in 2003 on the standing and implementation of corporate diplomacy in the 30 largest German companies listed in the Dax produced the following results:

- 80 % of the companies stated that they practised corporate diplomacy as a management function and core competence.
- Among corporate diplomacy managers, 40 % were lawyers, 30 % (former) senior government officials and 20 % (former) diplomats.
- The measures to promote future corporate diplomacy know-how are directed (at present) at only 10 % each of diplomats and graduates of diplomatic academies.[27]

In order to secure their collaborative advantage and survival in today's business environment transnational companies are building up a diplomatic staff for functions (such as complex interactions with civil, governmental and international institutions) that cannot be outsourced to public relations agencies. Increasingly transnational companies are hiring retired diplomats to advise senior management or to lead international affairs divisions within the company. This presents diplomats as well as academic institutes whose tasks and personnel are connected with diplomacy with a host of opportunities. This diplomatic and academic potential has not been tapped to a satisfactory degree to date.

In the age of global governance, governing is no longer solely in the hands of state players. Rather, government and civil society are called upon to enter into natural partnerships and creative alliances in order to master the new challenges of the present and future.

The growing trend towards transnational integration has led to a necessary paradigmatic change: the problems of globalization can no longer be mastered solely with traditional diplomacy but, rather, can only be resolved through participatory and cooperative interaction between politics, diplomacy, business and civil society.

Traditional diplomacy is therefore increasingly transforming from a purely state to a state/ non-state relationship and a political network between diplomacy and transnational companies is emerging. Corporate diplomacy can offer connecting elements and useful instruments within the scope of this transformation.

Today, diplomacy is conducted by many participants including diplomats. "New diplomats" are the regulators on the front lines of issues that were once the exclusive preserve of governmental policy but nowadays cannot be resolved by national authorities alone. Both work now side by side.

Transnational companies can be important partners in the realization of the UN goals of peace and development. The creation of jobs, incomes and social security, training and the transfer of know-how, foreign direct investment, trade and the resulting economic cooperation and integration can have a substantial impact in peacemaking. In this connection, voluntary codes of conduct drawn up by the companies themselves, by non-governmental organizations or by international organizations, codes of conduct which companies voluntarily respect as an expression of their overall societal responsibility extending beyond their existing legal obligations, take on greater significance.

References

[1] **Jessica T. Mathews**, Power Shift, in: Foreign Affairs Jan/Feb 1997, p.50

[2] **Heinrich Triepel**, Die auswärtige Politik der Privatpersonen, in: Zeitschrift für ausländisches öffentliches Recht, vol. 9 (1939/40), p. 6

[3] **George F. Kennan**, Diplomacy without diplomats?, in: Foreign Affairs Jan/Feb 1997, p. 204

[4] **Jean-François Bayart,** Le gouvernement du monde. Une critique politique de la globalisation, (Paris: Fayard 2004) p. 69ç

[5] **Jan Melissen**, Innovation in diplomatic practice, p. XIV

[6] **Thomas Risse-Kappen**, Bringing transnational relations back in, (Cambridge: Cambridge University Press 1995)

[7] **Susan Strange**, States, firms and diplomacy, in: International Affairs, January 1992, p. 10

[8] **Béatrice Hibou**, Privatising the state, (London: Hurst 2004), p. 95

[9] **Susan Strange**, The retreat of the state. The diffusion of power in the world economy, (Cambridge: Cambridge University Press 1996)
Wolfgang Reinicke, Global Public Policy. Governing without Government?, (Washington: Brookings Institution Press 1998), p. 52

[10] **Ulrich Steger**, Corporate Diplomacy (Chichester: Wiley&Sons 2003)

[11] **Wilfried Bolewski**, Modernes Management des diplomatischen Protokolls, in: Modernes Protokoll (Berlin: German Foreign Office 2004), p. 7

[12] **Michael Watkins/Mickey Edwards/Usha Thakrar**, Winning the influence game: Effective business strategies for managing governmental relations (New York: Wiley&Sons 2001), p.193

[13] **Michael Edwards / Simon Zadek**, Governing the provision of global public goods: the role and legitimacy of nonstate actors, in**: Inge Kaul / Pedro Conceicao / Katell Le Goulven / Ronald U. Mendoza (ed.)**, Providing global public goods, (Oxford: Oxford University Press 2003), p.200

[14] See the critical voices in: **The Economist** of 22 January 2005: A survey of corporate social responsibility. Earlier also **Milton Friedmann**, The social responsibility of business is to increase its profits, in: New York Times Magazine, September 13, 1970

[15] This tribunal was established pursuant to Clause 28 of the Deeds of Concession between the Government of the Libyan Arab Republic, on the one hand, and California Asiatic Oil Company and Texaco Overseas Petroleum Company, on the other hand.

[16] Texas Overseas Petroleum Co. & California Asiatic Oil Co. v. Libyan Arab Republic, in: International Legal Materials 17 (1978), p. 1. In 1970 the International Court of Justice extended the law relating to aliens to include companies. It states that the international law has to correspond to the continuous evolution in the field of diplomatic protection: Barcelona Traction, Light and Power Co. Ltd. (Belgium vs. Spain), Judgement of 5 February 1970, in: International Court of Justice, Reports of Judgements, Advisory Opinions and Orders, 1970, p.3.

[17] LaGrand Case (Germany v. United States of America), Judgement of 27 June 2001, in: International Legal Materials 40 (2001), p. 1069

[18] Ad Hoc Tribunal for Yugoslavia (1993), Ad Hoc Tribunal for Rwanda (1994), Special Court for Sierra Leone (2002), Khmer-Rouge-Tribunal

[19] **Daniel Thürer**, The emergence of Non-Governmental Organizations and Transnational Enterprises in international law and the changing role of the state, in: **Rainer Hoffmann/Nils Geissler (ed.)**, Non-State Actors as new subjects of international law (Berlin: Duncker & Humblot 1998) p. 46

[20] **Karsten Nowrot**, Legal consequences of globalization: The status of Non-Governmental Organizations under international law, in: Global Legal Studies Journal, vol. 6/ 1999, p.46

[21] **Fleur Johns**, The invisibility of the Transnational Corporation: An analysis of international law and legal theory, in: Melbourne University Law Review, vol. 19/1994, p.893

[22] **Daniel Thürer**, The emergence of Non-Governmental Organizations, p. 66

[23] **Claudia Kissling,** The legal status of NGOs in international governance and its relevance for the legimitacy of international organizations (Bremen: TranState Working Papers No. 38/2006)

[24] **Steve Charnovitz,** Nongovernmental Organizations and International Law, in: American Journal of International Law, vol. 100 (2006) p. 348 (355)

[25] **Claudia Kissling,** p. 24

[26] **Brian Hocking**, Catalytic Diplomacy: Beyond "Newness" and "Decline" in: **Melissen**, Innovation in Diplomatic Practice,
Richard Langhorne, The diplomacy of non-state actors, in: Diplomacy and Statecraft, vol. 16, 2005, p. 331,
James P. Muldoon, The diplomacy of business, in: Diplomacy and Statecraft, vol. 16, 2005, p. 341

[27] **Wilfried Bolewski**, Symbiose entre diplomatie et entreprises transnationales, in: Revue internationale et stratégique, No. 60, 2005/2006, p. 58
Wilfried Bolewski, Von den Multis lernen. Corporate Diplomacy: Wie sich die Außenpolitik vernetzt, in: Internationale Politik, 9/2005, p. 82

Chapter 8
Citizen diplomats and public relations diplomacy: popularization of diplomacy

Institutions and practices of diplomacy are spreading at the same rate as transnational relations are developing within a new global system. Change and transformation are therefore the dominant themes of modern diplomacy.

We have already developed the aspects of Para- und proto-diplomacy of substate entities, track-two diplomacy by non-governmental representatives and corporate diplomacy by transnational companies. Let us now turn to a further extension of diplomacy: citizen diplomats. Two basic types can be distinguished in practice:[1]

1) The citizen diplomat as a lobbyist or advocate of a particular international cause (for example humanitarian or political)

2) The citizen diplomat as an autonomous agent in international relations (for example world-renowned figures who act in a private capacity representing their own economic or political interests –celebrity diplomacy). From Marco Polo to Bill Gates and Ted Turner, business professionals have acted as diplomats and as a global force for good citizenship because of their cultural sensitivity to their own environment as well as to the world at large and the global enterprise they are heading.

This new relational paradigm is based on the following perceptions of politics:

- citizens as political actors capable of influencing the course of events
- civil society as the complex of associations that active citizens form and through which they interact with other groups (networking)
- politics as a cumulative, multilevel, open-ended process of continuous interaction involving these citizens and associations
- connections between citizens outside and inside government creating whole body politics. Politics is thus coming back into society.

The popularization of access to information has turned citizens into independent observers as well as assertive participants in globalized relations, and the new agenda of diplomacy has only added to the leverage of such groupings.[2] Globalization has taken foreign affairs out of the Chanceries and taken it into the heads and hands of the people.

This political concept of the twenty-first century has been called the "Citizen's Century"[3]. Citizen Diplomats can and should learn from modern diplomacy as practised by professional representatives of sovereign states. The parties learn, test and introduce practices that seem to ease or enhance the conduct of the relationships. These codes of conduct or principles correspond to those of traditional diplomacy.

All human activity and interchange involve some aspects of diplomacy in form of courtesy, respect, tact. This personal diplomacy corresponds, in fact, only to the rules of etiquette in social behaviour. They are neither legally nor morally required. Yet, there is some sense of obligation to perform these rules. On the other hand, there are the rules of international protocol, though not legally binding with legal sanctions, yet there violation can carry grave political consequences.

In 2005, a group of former diplomats has formed an organization called "Independent Diplomat" (ID) in London and New York which is consulting governments of non-recognized states such as Kosovo, Somaliland and Westsahara.

The relational paradigm and its actions of private diplomats on the international stage pose no real threat to the state system of diplomatic discourse but add to the mixed system of stakeholders within the international system. Since diplomacy emerges wherever individuals or groups conduct cross-border relations with one another, it is therefore not exclusively linked to the sovereign state system. Diplomatic communication, historically based on government-to-government and diplomat-to-diplomat interactions, has expanded to include government-to-people and people-to-people contacts.

Citizen diplomats can and should learn from modern diplomacy as practised by professional representatives of sovereign states and benefit from the knowledge and insight from social scientific research (sociology, psychology, anthropology, language and communication) on human behaviour.

Within some modern societies a new phenomenon of "public relations diplomacy" is appearing which results in a certain popularization and even vulgarization of diplomacy: Apart from traditional diplomatic titles modern society is creating more and more innovative pseudo-diplomatic denominations. Awarded sometimes to well-respected personalities and celebrities, they are seen as a way to interest the public via the media in commercial, charity or social purposes and actively promote these causes. The increasing use of pseudo diplomatic titles in the non-diplomatic world reflects the attraction the world of diplomacy exercises within the general public. The examples range from UNESCO-goodwill-Ambassador to beauty/beer/wine-Ambassadors. Since diplomacy is about representation the wide variety of purposes such as advertisement for products, public entities, cities or humanitarian organizations also exemplifies the popularization of diplomatic titles in modern society. Traditional diplomatic and consular titles are legally protected by the Vienna Conventions on Diplomatic and Consular Relations in connection with domestic law which should combat against any misuse of diplomatic or consular institutions and prevent any pretexting in the diplomatic arena.[4]

The following criteria can serve as guidelines distinguishing between traditional and pseudo-diplomatic titles:

- a genuine state representation
- a diplomatic/consular mission
- the authority to legally bind a state or an International Organization.

References

1 **Paul Sharp**, Making Sense of Citizen Diplomats, in: **Jönsson/Langhorne**, Diplomacy, vol.3, p. 343

2 **Jan Melissen**, The new public diplomacy. Soft power in international relations, (Houndmills: Palgrave Macmillan 2005) p.3

3 **Harald H. Saunders**, Politics is about relationship. A blueprint for the Citizen's Century, (New York: Palgrave Macmillan 2005) p. 20, 85

4 **Wilfried Bolewski**, Misuse and protection of diplomatic and consular titles, in: The Australian Law Journal 2003, p.750

Part III
Towards a diplomatic corporate identity?

Chapter 9
The importance of an international diplomatic culture

From a practitioner's point of view diplomatic culture can be evaluated as the accumulated communicative and representational practices, rules, and institutions devised to improve relations and avoid war between interacting politicial entities.[1] They are to be separated from the legal obligations of international law (customary or treaty such as the UN Charter) and reach beyond those.

Although processes of cultural exchange and interaction have shaped the emergence of modernity in distinctive ways, they are still largely perceived as an expansion of western modernity. The spectrum of non-western responses to social- economic, political and cultural models and world order largely influenced by Western Europe and the United States ranges from unreserved adoption and cautious adaptation to the formulation of alternative vision of governance at the local, national, regional and global levels. Specific notions of identity and of social-cultural cohesion seem to call for different institutions and modes of governance, reflecting not just cultural preferences but also economic interests and specific geopolitical constellations. While some of these models assert validity for a particular community or society only, others claim universal validity competing with western models. Irrespective of the claims and perceptions of their advocates, these models do not develop in isolation, but result from complex patterns of interaction with other cultural traditions, visions and practices.

It is the relevance of culture and the cultural embeddedness of governance which determines identity, authenticity and social cohesion in globalized relations. Language is pivotal to this cultural identity.[2]

The tendency of globalization has brought about a certain degree of cultural convergence to the point of homogenization but also shown some areas of ethnic or religious polarizations. In lack of common identity-in-the-making we are therefore far from a nascent truly global culture referring to collective model of evaluative and cognitive standards and values.

The determining procedural factor in diplomatic negotiations are very often the cultural differences ("cultural gap") and resulting discordances between the negotiating parties. These "cultural gaps" are often at first detectable at a linguistic level. Culture is the underlying dimension of any international interaction. Therefore, the understanding of culture as a complex of attributes subsuming every area of social life provides a key to the successful outcome of negotiations.[3]

Diplomats (as other well travelled elites) have to be knowledgeable and sensible to other cultures and their context in the foreign domestic scene (customs, manners, form of social organisation). Different cultures produce varying international negotiating styles (verbal and explicit): the Anglo-Saxon rationality of give-and-take fosters the problem-solving model. Other, especially non-western, approaches view a more long-term relationship and are concerned with consideration of symbolism and status. This is a more communicatory, face-saving style.[4] Both styles may, at times but not necessarily, merge in the tendency of cultural conversion.

The similar or common training (in national or international diplomatic schools) and the uniform code of conduct may create a sense of belonging to an international professional community. Indeed, there are many behavioural similarities in this profession (especially among neighbouring countries or regional or political groupings such as the EU) which create an "esprit de corps" (corporate spirit of professional ethics, a common stock of ideas and values, code of conduct[5]). Nevertheless, cross-cultural differences can also play a role in diplomatic understandings and proceedings. In bilateral as well as multilateral diplomatic dealings cultural differences (customs, manners, forms of social organisation but especially intellectual mind-sets) can lead to a cultural gap impinging on the diplomatic process. From a practitioner's point of view, the way out of a possible dead-lock due to cultural differences and misunderstandings is the search by all partners in the diplomatic intercourse for a common ground of values or experiences (third platform, agreed framework) from which to carry out the interaction constructively.

What is common to the development of diplomacy derives not only from similar patterns for the administration of foreign affairs but also from their participation in a common field of diplomatic action. What differentiate them are those domestic characteristics that have produced the modern, independent, sovereign state. Institutional differences reflect the size, power, governmental structure and political leadership in each state. Though shared international experiences create common forms, diplomacy developing within a separate politicial system will keep its own distinctive and variable cultural characteristics.[6]

In the final analysis, it is the diversity of national interests which poses a natural political delimitation to any communality within the diplomatic profession. The personal friendship among colleagues will normally be superseded by the hardcore interests one has to promote and defend as a successful and credible diplomat.

There is no doubt a gradual assimilation of national and regional styles of diplomacies which is also promoted by the common work in International Organizations and through multilateral diplomacy. But from a practitioner's point of view it would be illusory to talk presently about a distinct/single diplomatic culture or corporate identity,[7] also because contemporary diplomacy is going through a process of adaptation, changing conditions and the introduction of outside participants. The fact that diplomatic practices and values are often transgressed in pursuit of national interest[8] remains a strong argument for the disputed existence and against the general acceptance of a diplomatic culture.

References

[1] A broader definiton is given by **Geoffrey Wiseman,** Pax Americana: Bumping into diplomatic culture, in: International Studies Perspectives, vol. 6 (2005), p. 409

[2] **Leigh Oakes**, Language and National Identity, (Amsterdam/Philadelphia: John Benjamins Publishing Company 2001)
Thomas M. Franck, The empowered self. Law and society in the age of individualism, (Oxford: Oxford University Press 1999), p. 95

[3] **Raymond Cohen**, Negotiating Across Cultures. International Communication in an Interdependent World (Washington: United Institute of Peace Press 2002), 3rd revised edition

[4] **Raymond Cohen**, Negotiating Across Cultures, p. 216

[5] **Hedley Bull,** The Anarchical Society: A study of order in world politics, (New York: Columbia University Press 3rd ed. 2002) p. 304, 160

[6] **Zara Steiner (ed.),** The Times survey of foreign ministries of the world (London: Times Books 1982) p. 11

[7] **Christer Jönsson**, Essence of Diplomacy, p. 39 seems to detect a diplomatic subculture due to:
– shared symbols and references
– mutual expectations, agreed-upon rules, regulations and procedures
– formal organizations.
From a practical point of view, cultural and political differences and interests among diplomats will prevail over shared beliefs, values and discursive practices.

[8] **Geoffrey Wiseman,** p. 416

Chapter 10
The relevance of language

The universe of discourse of diplomacy remains cosmopolitan. The art of diplomacy is not to outmanoeuvre the opponent/partner but to convince him of common interests or the disadvantages of his own position.[1] Since international relations are mostly conducted as communicative interaction language is the essential instrument and tool of diplomacy.[2] Language is the dominant medium of negotiation. It conveys ones own ideas and concepts, and offers the means of understanding the thoughts and expectations of the other side. Language is not only a neutral medium of representation; it is also actively involved in the constitution of legal and political reality.

Language is therefore the bridge for communication which leads the way from the simple motivation to interact to real cooperation. This socialization process of communication, argumentation and persuasion concerns argumentative discourses in the Habermasian sense.[3] Language as a common media of official international communication is a perfect tool and significant part of diplomatic equipment in the exercise of political influence, power and dominance.[4]

Unfortunately, the function, importance and even central role of language in diplomacy have in the past found little or no attention.[5]

Among the diplomatic languages English is the most popular, because it is the first choice amongst the masses and the elite alike. In addition to the 375 million native speakers (including the 53 member states of the Commonwealth), it has been suggested that 1.1 billion people know English as a second or foreign language (some only at the lower level of "globish"), outnumbering the native speakers by 3 to 1. 51 % of Europeans speak English as their native or as a foreign language. With a great tolerance in linguistic variations English as a global language has become the language of power and prestige and thereby an international gate-keeper to social and economic progress. The current dominance of English as a world language is undisputed. It plays an official or working role in most international organizations and fora.

The traditional strength of French as a diplomatic language (the former lingua franca of diplomacy) is linked to the educational and cultural prestige attached to it by the 63 partner-states of the Francophonie (49 member states, 4 associated states, and 10 observer states) and to the role of French diplomacy. Its linguistic role can be defined as

- generating a positive French identity,
- promoting French as a language of international mediation and
- accepting a more polycentric approach to French-speaking culture.

Recent surveys[6] count world-wide 112 million "francophones réels", 60 million "francophones occasionnels" and 110 million "françisants". More important than the numbers of French-speakers is the fact that French has become an instrument of social stratification. The French passed political power in their colonies to an elite group they had created based on their own culture. Today, the children and grandchildren of an earlier French-trained elite grow up in a cultivated, virtually French home environment. French forms a common bond of this elite.

German ranges as the most wide-spread native tongue in Europe (18 % of the European population, mostly in Germany, Austria, Switzerland, Belgium and Italy) and the second most important foreign language.[7]

For a diplomat it is also advisable to be able to use the local language of the country in order to

- understand the feeling of the people,
- show them courtesy and build trust (informal trust is culturally defined by the values and norms that allow people to communicate and deal with others who share those values),
- gain the respect of the people and admission to the heart of the nation and
- receive reliable information on local conditions and sentiment and be able to interpret it.

Thus, multilingualism is an essential feature of diplomacy. The variety of culture in Europe for example leads to a diversified language policy in the European Union. Europe's linguistic diversity is at the core of its identity. Multilingualism should seek to promote respect for diversity and tolerance with a view to preventing the emergence of active or passive conflicts between different language communities in the Member States. The objective is the following regime ("mother tongue plus 2"):

- the personal, social- and cultural identity-bearing national language as native tongue and
- the two traditional languages of diplomacy (English and French) plus
- additional working languages.

In 2007, the European Union has installed a Commissioner for Multilingualism to promote this policy. This strategy of divergence in convergence is an effective means of generating positive common identities.

Language as such has always been more than a means of communication; it has also assumed a political role.[8] Power and even dominance are played out through language. Diplomacy is primarily words that prevent the reaching for arms. The power of language rests on the fact that it contains ideas which are more permanent than matter. The word of a diplomat constitutes an intentional political act. Language can lead to better communication, better cross-cultural understanding, better negotiation and document drafting, thus to better diplomacy in the sense of peace-promoting.

Decisive/dominating knowledge as a human resource (Herrschaftswissen)[9] is encapsulated in language. Language expresses, creates, exerts and maintains influence and power in politics. Language is therefore also the key/tool to dismantle any such dominance. A dialogue free of dominance presupposes equal language mastery by all interacting parties.

All language comes with hidden meanings and intentions, historical and political context, legal precedents. In order to find these hidden meanings the diplomat needs a broad understanding of the context of the situation. In diplomatic negotiations concerning matters of law, jurisdiction or administration it is an advantage and at times even a prerequisite to have sound linguistic knowledge and command of the constitutional and organizational background of the respective societies in order to build on common terms of reference.

In comparison to the own mastery of language the practice of third party interpretation can only play a secondary role due to

- loss of time
- difficulty of translating certain idioms (with regard to cultural differences) and
- lack of behavioural nuances and confidence.

In any case, confidence by both parties in the interpreter is essential for his diplomatic endeavour. At times of great tensions in a diplomatic conversation participants tend to prefer to speak even in a language that they do not really master rather than pass through an interpreter.

References

[1] **Henry Kissinger**, Years of Upheaval, (Boston, Massachusetts: Little Brown 1982) p. 214

[2] **Harald Müller**, Internationale Beziehungen als kommunikatives Handeln, in: Zeitschrift für Internationale Beziehungen, I / 1994, p.15

[3] **Jürgen Habermas**, Theorie des kommunikativen Handelns,(Frankfurt/Main: Suhrkamp 1981) 2 volumes
Thomas Risse, Let's Argue, p. 7 (see page 26)

[4] **Pierre Bourdieu**, Language and Symbolic Power, (Cambridge: Polity Press 1991)
Constanze Villar, Le discours diplomatique, (Paris: L'Harmattan 2006)

[5] **Alexander Ostrower**, Language, law, and diplomacy, (Philadelphia: University of Pennsylvania Press 1965) vol. II, p. 806
Wilhelm G. Grewe, Die Sprache der Diplomatie, (Hamburg: Freie Akademie der Künste 1967)

[6] **Olivier Pierrot,** Die Rolle der Francophonie in den franko-afrikanischen Beziehungen (Berlin: Wissenschaftlicher Verlag Berlin 2006), p. 47

[7] **Alexander Ostrower**, Language, law, and diplomacy, vol. II, p. 806
Wilhelm G. Grewe, Die Sprache der Diplomatie

[8] **Harald Haarmann**, Die Sprachenwelt Europas, (Frankfurt: Wissenschaftliche Buchgesellschaft 1993) p. 80

[9] **Thomas Finkenstaedt / Konrad Schröder**, Sprachenschranken statt Zollschranken? (Essen: Stifterverband für die Deutsche Wissenschaft 1991) 2nd ed., p. 9

Part IV
Globalized relations and the law

Chapter 11
Private authority in transnational relations

The complex phenomenon of globalization is a process of social change in the world as a whole. It is composed of the following, at times contradictory, dimensions[1]:

- interdependence in a largely unregulated space at the international level
- fragmentation in groups promoting their own interests
- in some market-orientated systems, unification possibly leading to uniformity (unity of disunity)
- homogenization and
- diversification.

They present challenges as well as opportunities for social movements on a global scale.

State and government structures are not the only ones promoting transformative social change. In transnational civil societies with their associational networks social change movements foster a continuous process of transboundary interactions. They use new modes of governance and wield influence over social, political and economic developments and even over the creation of new regulatory norms, whether they will be accepted as legitimate and authoritative or not. These social change movements use their positions of authority within their transboundary networks to set the international agenda. They make use of their influence and access to diplomatic and public relations skills to promote their interests and causes in order to bring about change in the policies and practices of governments and International Organizations.

This globalization with the subsequent rise of decentralized network-organizations provides an opportunity and advantage for non-state participants in law-interpreting, law-implementing and eventually law-making. The varieties of non-state participants operating today enjoy an increasing relevance as major actors in organizing the international system. As former marginals of society they now become subjects as well as objects of considerable authority in their relationships with the state. They can promote any issue of concern and put pressure on governments and International Organizations to push for normative change. With their private authority non-state participants enter into a new correlation with traditional state-actors allowing for competitive advantages of either the state or the non-state actor in the management of governance arrangements.[2]

While states are used to negotiate as sovereign actors, globalization can undermine this authority of the state through new forms of private authority by non-state participants on the basis of market or interest imperatives.

Surely, the state legitimized by society represents the collective law-making. But he can also delegate this regulatory function to a more efficient private sector. Without such delegation of power, non-state participants can develop rules legitimated only by their stakeholders. They are able to respond with greater flexibility to rapid change than states.

States provide public goods within their fiscal constraints; non-state participants have access to their additional private finances. With their specialized resources they can participate – in concert with or separate from state mechanisms – in the provision of public goods.

With regard to enforcement, the state enjoys his legitimate monopoly, whereas non-state participants provide leverage through interdependence.

In reality, laws produced by states and self-regulatory institutions generated by non-state actors often complement or substitute each other. They can even form a symbiotic relationship.

The process of globalization has transformed the nature and character of non-state participation with respect to the distribution and legitimacy of power. Non-state participants produce their authority quite independently from the state. The emergence of this private authority can at times be seen as an efficient solution to problems of collective decision-making and as a response to particular social, economic, political and technological contexts. Occasionally, endowing private participants with regulative authority can provide more efficiency gains than relying solely on state authority.

This regulative authority operates through a sense of obligation rather than coercion. It consists of decision-making over an issue and is accepted as legitimate by their participants. When states have been unable to provide effective structure of governance private actors can step in. Though private participants lack the authority to prescribe and enforce state laws (unless delegated to them) and though they have no legal personality under international law to engage in law creation and enforcement they can in fact govern over issue areas, both at the state and at the international level. Their governance takes place either in the absence of or in coordination with state governments.

The transnational civil society practises a "bottom-up" approach to democracy which can even include norms of transparency and accountability in its social cooperative relationships. In their transformative social change they, too, aim for democratic entitlement.

In globalized relations the regulatory power extends beyond the government and its agents into the realm of civil society. A growing number of participants other than the state appear to have taken on authoritative roles and functions in the international system. The difference between authority and power lies with the legitimacy of claims of authority. Legitimacy implies some form of normative, uncoerced consent or recognition of authority on the part of the regulated which amounts to the normative belief by the participants that a rule ought to be obeyed. Whereas power requires obedience, authority is based on trust.

As the number of participants in foreign affairs is growing the range of international issues and topics dealt with by them in a complementary, cooperative or supplementary way is increasing as well. They extend from domestic to transnational matters and issue areas. These contacts take place in a vertical or horizontal direction; they favour collective action within an international social order upgrading the common interests. This proliferation of international authorities and the ensuing multiplication of engagements by state and non-state participants and among non-state actors create a new network of obligations.

References

[1] **Wolfgang Reinicke,** Tugging at the sleeves of politicians, (Gütersloh: Bertelsmann Foundation Publishers 1996), p. 13

[2] **A. Claire Cutler/Virginia Haufler/Tony Porter,** The contours and significance of private authority in international affairs, in: **A. Claire Cutler/Virginia Haufler/Tony Porter (ed.),** Private authority and international affairs, (Albany: State University of New York Press 1999), p. 333

Chapter 12
Transnational regime as soft law

This innovation of sectoral and functional regulatory structures and mechanisms certainly has a moral, social, economic or political background, but it is questionable if it also has any genuine normative character. In comparison to the broader category of norms, law has a more formal status. All rules and norms that operate in international relations are not necessarily legal in nature. International law increasingly forms the substance of international relations. Nearly all diplomatic and political issues have a crucial legal dimension to them. As globalized relations develop towards a fuller acceptance of transantional cooperation and, ultimately, the existence of a global society, the role of international law in providing a framework for such developments will grow.

International law matters because of the range and numbers of participants in international relations addressing it. In view of the potential participation of non-state actor in the formation of international norms there is a need for an interdisciplinary re-examination of the relational, discursive and constitutive functions of norm formation in international law in the light of international social change. The interests and identities of non-state actors participate in the new distribution of political power in our changing world. It creates a mutually constructive relationship between the new participants and existing international structures and their norms.

The non-state actors adopt nonbinding normative instruments for effective, efficient and flexible responses to common problems. They can signon, participate, and be targets of regulations which are faster to adopt and easier to change.

With the disaggregating of public authority from the state to private participants a new layer of intersubjective transnational structure is emerging. This normative network positions itself between the domestic legal order and the international legal order. Its sectorialized and decentralized structure brings a novelty to the international legal order[1] and is occupying a normative layer of its own: Such a transnational regime is self-regulatory and draws from national law as well as general principles of international law. Together with international law it forms part of the new global law. But, these international regulations also directly or indirectly affect domestic options of regulation in their relationship between transnational regimes and domestic legal system. Due to their humanitarian, economic or ecological character these regimes develop shared values but basically lack structured community institutions.

At the same time, the principles of international law are being borrowed by international corporations and thus intruding into the dealings and relations of private companies and non-governmental organizations. These actions and policies have immediate impact upon the daily lives of many people. They gradually become of primary importance while the state often resign to intervene and control these activities. This vast web of non-state international dealings also entails a secularization of international law.[2] The three layers of international, regime and domestic norms become closely interrelated.

It seems realistic and necessary to consider the role and activities of the non-state participants in the context of international norm generation in as much as they practise international principles such as democracy, accountability and legitimacy.[3] Their practices are normative expressions. They reflect the degree in which a civil society has absorbed particular international norms. Their behaviour adds to the norm-proliferation, norm-generation and norm-application by both state and non-state actors. Certainly, non-state participants cannot be put on an equal footing with states in the process of international customary law formation but actions and behaviour of non-state actors can influence the interpretation and social development of international customary law. The traditional approach is that for the development of international customary law according to article 38 para. 1 lit b of the Statute of the International Court of Justice ("a general practice accepted as law") only state practice and opinio iuris is acceptable. Yet, other actors (such as non-governmental organizations, transnational coprorations and civil society groups) have gained considerable influence in shaping the international legal landscape. Eventually, all society-members and regime-actors can be authors of customary law because they are the sources of its authority.[4] Therefore, it is foreseeable that in the future not only the behaviour of states but also that of non-state actors of international relations could be taken into account as a normative corrective. This would correspond to their increasing impact on international relations.[5] Even though such customary rule has not been established due to a lack of a general and consistent practice followed out of a sense of legal obligation by the participants, it seems that such a principle is indeed emerging.

With the structure of the international system the role that legal rules play in international relations is also changing. The process of creating legal rules will be fundamentally altered. General international law will come about through the many interactions of the multiple international actors. Therefore, the practice of the entire panoply of actors will have to be examined and evaluated.[6]

At the same time there is a dynamic of international norms becoming internalized into domestic law. International reality clearly proves that states and non-state participants, at times, are entering into legal relationships governed by rules of international law. But in multi-layered relations these contacts mostly fall outside of the traditional categories of public or private international law and are often described as self-regulatory or (legally not binding) soft law[7] (as civil society practice), though it lacks two characteristics of law: to be directly enforceable and to lead to legal sanctions. The normative content of soft law comes from the consensual nature of the instruments operating on the basis of mutual trust and reciprocity. This includes self-imposed codes of conduct, guidelines, understandings and international standards leading to a normatization of transnational relations. These regimes of informal rules, norms and procedures (as normative categories), which help to shape the performance of international actors, are interpreted and applied not through formal mechanism of adjudication or arbitration but through social discourse and argument under the watchful eye of public opinion. These patterns of regulated behaviour form part of the broader fabric of international social norms. These norms are used in making decisions and in communicating the basis of those choices to a wider audience.[8] They emerge from the interaction of participants and a pattern of expectations about appropriate behaviour. These norms will continue to grow and regulate more and more aspects of international life, and in increasing detail. The significant advantages of soft law are that it is more easily attained than hard law, it provides procedures for dealing with uncertainties, it facilitates compromise among state and non-state actors and it can thus smoothly reshape international politics.

Surely, they do not have the character of legal prescriptions by the authority of the state, which leads to the question if they fall into a legal vacuum. On the other hand, their explicit, voluntary and regulatory nature and impact in transnational relations makes them the subject of an international regime defined by problem-solving effectiveness, social acceptance and stabilizing resilience. Furthermore, these informal norms and regulations are principally adhered to by all participants and stake-holders (network norms) on the basis of common or mutual interest and the expectation of reciprocity under the accepted concept and continuous process of governance.

Presently, there exists a continuum from hard law through various forms of soft law. While the borderline between legally binding rules and legally not-binding regulatory provisions is still to be determined in the international system it seems realistic within the process of civilization and legalization of transnational relations and the apparent constitutionalization of international law to acknowledge these regulatory provisions the status of relative functional normativity as a legal basis in international law. This would correspond to the tendency of legal pluralism[9] in the emerging international community. In a pluralistic legal system, states are only one relevant factor in the law-making and law-abiding process. Since the process of globalization does also have an impact on the development of international law, the practice of non-state participants should not be excluded from the assessment of this law.[10] But, it is due to the flexibility and adaptability of these new regulatory provisions to fast changing circumstances of globalization that, so far, they have not reached the stage of their own formal conceptualization, institutionalization or legalization.

These normative influences of coordinated social action shape international society but the status and sanctions of legal norms in an institutional framework are not necessarily accorded to them. It is perceivable that widely recognised transnational regimes could generate the acceptance of emerging legal norms through the particular strength of legal rationality and contribute to international change.[11] The considerable recourse to and compliance with informal social norms and voluntary, concontractual understanding and nonbinding norms may represent a maturing of the international system.[12]

Any discussion about the normative character of soft law and international regimes leads to the problem of compliance and implementation.[13] The overseeing of such norms can theoretically be evaluated by monitoring, control, enforcement and sanctioning for violations. But practical compliance in this context relies solely on self-regulation and self-control by its stake-holders and their responsive partners.

All the more uncertain is, at present, the possibility of their judicial implementation and review outside the established structures of private and public international law.[14] One has to state and accept that within the proliferation and privatization of foreign policy these innovative forms and structures are at best subject to political scrutiny (governmental or parliamentary) for abuses and risks but not to genuine judicial review. Because of their informal character these rules are not subject to sanctions or redress by the state. The overall state control over these dynamic and proliferating international regimes is therefore limited.

References

1 **Christian Walter**, Constitutionalizing (inter)national governance – Possibilities for and limits to the development of an international constitutional law, in: German Yearbook of International Law vol. 44 (2001), p.170
Charles-Albert Morand (ed.), Le droit saisi par la mondialisation (Bruxelles: Editions de l'Université de Bruxelles 2001), p. 97

2 **Vaughan Lowe,** The politics of law-making. Are the method and character of norm creating changing?, in: **Michael Byers (ed.)**, The role of law in international politics, Essays in international relations and international law (Oxford: Oxford University Press 2000), p. 221

3 **Philip Kunig,** Das Völkerrecht und die Interessen der Bevölkerung, in: **Pierre-Marie Dupuy/Bardo Fassbender/Malcolm N. Shaw/Karl-Peter Sommermann (ed.)**, Common Values in International Law. Essays in Honour of Christian Tomuschat, (Kehl: N.P. Engel Verlag 2006), p. 377

4 **Vaughan Lowe,** in: **Michael Byers (ed.),** p. 219
Stephen J. Toope, Emerging patterns of governance and international law, in: **Michael Byers (ed.),** p. 93
Philipp Allott, The concept of international law, in: **Michael Byers (ed.),** p. 77

5 **Stephen Hobe**, Die Zukunft des Völkerrechts im Zeitalter der Globalisierung – Perspektiven der Völkerrechtsentwicklung im 21. Jahrhundert, in: Archiv des Völkerrechts vol. 37 (1999), p.253
Carolin F. Hillmanns, Transnationale Unternehmen und Menschenrechte. Eine Studie zu den ersten beiden Prinzipien des Global Compact, Diss. Zürich 2004

6 **Anthony Clark Arend,** Legal rules and international society, (New York: Oxford University Press 1999), p. 177 (183)

7 **Marie-Claude Smouts,** La coopération internationale: de la coexistence à la gouvernance mondiale, in: **Marie-Claude Smouts (ed.)**, Les nouvelles relations internationales. Pratiques et théories, (Paris: Presses de Sciences Po 1998), p. 135
Kenneth W. Abbott/Duncan Snidal, Hard and soft law in international governance, in: International Organization vol. 54 no. 3 (2000) p. 421, 450
Karsten Nowrot, Nun sag, wie hast du's mit den Global Players? Fragen an die Völkerrechtsgemeinschaft zur internationalen Rechtsstellung transnationaler Unternehmen, in: Die Friedens-Warte 79 (2004), p. 119

8 **Christian Reus-Smit (ed.)**, The politics of international law, (Cambridge: Cambridge University Press 2004), p. 40

9 **Math Noortmann,** Non-state actors in international law, in: **Bas Arts/Math Noortmann/Bob Reinalda (ed.),** Non-state actors in international relations (Aldershot: Ashgate 2001), p. 59

10 **Karsten Kronit/Volker Schneider,** Global governance through private organizations, in: Governance: An International Journal of Policy and Administration, vol. 12, no. 3, July 1999, p. 243

[11] **Jutta Brunnée/Stephen J. Toope**, International law and constructivism: Elements of an interactional theory of international law, in: Columbia Journal of Transnational Law vol. 39 (2000) p. 19

[12] **Dinah Shelton,** Normative Hierarchy in International Law, in: American Journal of International Law, vol. 100 (2006), p.291 (322)

[13] **Julie Mertus,** Considering nonstate actors in the new millennium: Toward expanded participation in norm generation and norm application, in: New York University Journal of International Law and Politics, vol. 32:2 (2000), p. 537
Richard Little, International Regimes, in: **John Baylis/Steve Smith (ed.)**, The globalization in world politics. An introduction to international relations, (Oxford: Oxford University Press 3rd edition 2005), p. 372

[14] For the judicialization of soft law see the "half-truths" of **José E. Alvarez**, The new dispute settlers: (Half) truths and consequences, in: Texas International Law Journal vol. 38 (2003), p. 405
Montserrat Cuchillo, From sovereignty to decentralization, European integration and global governance, in: David J. Eaton (ed.), The end of sovereignty? A transatlantic perspective, (Hamburg: LIT Verlag 2006), p. 97 (114)

Chapter 13
Judicial review of governmental diplomacy

I. Public international law of state immunity

Whereas private authority in foreign affairs generally escapes the legal system of judicial review, the public authority of the state is principally subject to public international law in its foreign policy decisions by the executive. But its legal control by foreign courts is, first of all, guided and limited by the international regime of state immunity.

In public international law, state immunity is the right not to be submitted to the exercise of foreign jurisdiction. It is derived from two important concepts mentioned in Article 2 I of the UN-Charter:

- sovereignty and
- equality of states

A state is legally supreme within its own boundaries. As an international legal entity it has the power to make laws within the sphere of its influence (suprema potestas). Due to the legal equality of the state the sovereign and his agents are immune to the judgements of other nations (par in parem non habet iudicium). The purpose of state immunity is to safeguard the ability of states to discharge their functions without foreign interference, to protect their dignity and to maintain and facilitate international relations.

State immunity is the product of a conflict between two international law principles, sovereign equality and adjudicatory jurisdiction. State immunity exists with respect to certain core state conduct as an exception to the overriding principle of adjudicatory jurisdiction.

Under the historical concept of absolute sovereignty in their relations with other states unrestricted sovereign immunity followed. Nowadays state immunity is restricted in the following ways:

- Immunity ratione personae protects mainly the most important representatives and decision-makers of a state (acting on behalf of the state during the term of office)
- Immunity ratione materiae shields every incumbent or former state official but only with regard to official conduct. Here a differentiation between official acts (acta iure imperii, acts – whether legal or illegal – ultra vires – committed for official purposes) and private acts (acta iure gestionis, commercial or personal undertakings) must be made. This differentiation is applied on the basis of functionality and nature of the act, not its motivation.

For the effective protection of certain human rights an exception from immunity is made by modern international law in cases of core crimes (such as genocide, crimes against humanity, torture, slavery, and racial discrimination). These norms have achieved jus cogens status. These layers of the international value system are in a process of constant evolution.

This conceptional definition of state immunity as a traditional sovereign state right in submission to the modern concept of nonderogable ius cogens for certain individual rights is in accordance with the hierarchy of values of the international community and reflects state practice as well as opinio iuris.[1]

II. Comparative study of domestic legal systems

The international law concept of state immunity finds its application within the varying systems of domestic law and the control of foreign relations in national courts. The different historical and constitutional concepts of judicial review of executive decisions relating to foreign relations shall be the subject of a comparative survey of the legal systems and state practices in the United Kingdom, the United States, France and Germany.[2]

All these avoidance doctrines discussed below are judge-made.

This study will deal with the dichotomy of politics and the rule of law in the field of foreign relations. The crucial question is whether executive acts of diplomacy are gaining more and more independence from social, parliamentary and eventually also judicial control or whether the international constitutionalization leads to a strengthening of the judiciary to the point of a judicialization of foreign affairs. To what extent can the judiciary control the legality of the conduct of foreign affairs by the executive?

References

1 **Ernest K. Bankas,** The state immunity controversy in international law. Private suits against sovereign states in domestic courts, (Berlin-Heidelberg-New York: Springer 2005)

Lee M. Caplan, State immunity, human rights, and jus cogens: A critique of the normative hierarchy theory, in: The American Journal of International Law vol. 97 (2003) p.741

Jürgen Bröhmer, State immunity and the violation of human rights (The Hague: Martinus Nijhoff Publishers 1997)

Hazel Fox, The law of state immunity (Oxford: Oxford University Press 2002)

Christian Tomuschat, L'immunité des états en cas de violations graves des droits de l'homme, in: Revue Générale de Droit International Public 2005, p.51

Beatrix Real, Staatenimmunität und Menschenrechte (Berlin: Logos 2004)

2 For further comparative studies of other countries see:

Frédérique Rueda, Le contrôle de l'activité du pouvoir exécutif par le juge constitutionnel. Les exemples français, allemand et espagnol (Paris: Librairie Générale de Droit et de Jurisprudence 2000),

Hélène Tourard, L'internationalisation des constitutions nationales, (Paris: Librairie Générale de Droit et de Jurisprudence 2000)

Theodor Schweisfurth/Ralf Alleweldt, The position of international law in the domestic legal orders of central and eastern European countries, in: German Yearbook of International Law, vol. 40 (1997), p.164

Guigo Wang, Une analyse nouvelle de la doctrine de "l'Acte d'État" appliquée notamment à la Court of Final Appeal de Hong-Kong, in: Revue de la recherche juridique – droit prospectif, vol. 22 (1997) p. 395

Pierre Michel Eisemann (ed.), L'intégration du droit international et communautaire dans l'ordre juridique national: Etude de la pratique en Europe, (The Hague: Kluwer 1996)

Benedetto Conforti (rapporteur), The activities of national judges and the international relations of their state, Yearbook of the Institute of International Law, vol. 65 (1993) Part I, p.327

Eyal Benvenisti, Judicial misgivings regarding the application of international law: An analysis of attitudes of national courts, in: European Journal of International Law, vol. 4 (1993), no. 2, p. 159

R. Ergec, La doctrine de l'Act of State et la jurisprudence belge, in: Revue de droit international et de droit comparé, vol. 61 (1984), p. 61

Prosper Weil, Le contrôle par les tribunaux nationaux de la licéité internationale des actes des états étrangers, in: Annuaire Français de Droit International 1977, p. 9.

Elihu Lauterpacht/John G. Collier, Individual rights and the state in foreign affairs, (New York: Praeger 1977)

D.S.A. Al Issa, Les théories relatives aux actes de gouvernement en droit français et dans les droits de certains pays arabes, Thèse Rennes, 1980

D. Voinesco, La théorie des actes de gouvernement en droit public roumain, Thèse Paris, 1932 (Les Éditions Internationales)

1. Act of State doctrine in the United Kingdom

With regard to justiciability of the conduct of foreign relations a clear distinction is drawn by the judiciary between acts of a foreign state (Act of Foreign State) and acts of their own government (Act of State).

a) U.K. Act of Foreign State

The international relations principle of act of foreign state was clearly spelled out by Halsbury's Laws of England:[1]

"Of Foreign Governments: The official acts of every state or potentate whose independence has been recognised by the Crown, and of their authorised agents, are acts of State. No action can be brought in respect of such acts, even where the agent is a British subject, and where, in carrying out the act of State, he is committing an offence against English law [...] These matters, it is submitted, belong in strictness to private or public international law, and depend upon considerations different from acts of State in the point of view of municipal law."

In other words, these are official acts of every sovereign state (and its authorized representatives) whose independence is recognized by the Crown.

State immunity is a creature of international law and operates as a plea in bar to the jurisdiction of the national court, whereas the Act of State doctrine is a rule of domestic law which holds the national court incompetent to adjudicate upon the lawfulness of the sovereign acts of foreign state.[2] The court may indeed hear a case, but it is denied the opportunity to review the validity of a foreign act. The merits of the case must be decided independent of the validity of the act which must be assumed to be valid.

About the interaction between the two institutions it has been stated:[3]

"The principle of sovereign immunity and non-justiciability (i.e. Act of State) overlap in practice. But in legal theory they are separate. State immunity, including head of state immunity, is a principle of international law. It creates a procedural bar to the jurisdiction of the court. Logically therefore it comes first. Non-justiciability is a principle of private international law. It goes to the substance of the issue to be decided. It requires the court to withdraw from adjudication on the grounds that the issues are such as the court is not competent to decide. State immunity being a procedural bar to the jurisdiction of the court, can be waived by the state. Non-justiciability being a substantive bar to adjudication cannot."

Immunity prevents the acceptance of a case by the court; the Act of State doctrine prevents the intrusive scrutiny and its judgement.[4]

The Act of State doctrine is defined as a common law principle of uncertain application which prevents the English courts from examining the legality of certain acts performed in the exercise of sovereign authority within a foreign country.[5] It can be derogated by Parliament as has been done for torture in the Criminal Justice Act of 1998 and it finds its general limits – as in the principle of state immunity – at the higher ranks of ius cogens (violation grave de normes fondamentales des droits de l'homme, règles impératives qui constituent le fondement de l'ordre juridique international).[6] This application of the international value system (ius cogens) in the domestic legal order shows the overlapping in content between the two layers.

The English conflict of laws accepts also the local public policy to override foreign acts of state.[7] This concerns the courts evaluation of the foreign governmental motives to be acceptable and not offensive and filters out only the most egregious acts (ultra vires).

The reasoning behind the Act of State doctrine revolves more around political motives, purposes and expediencies rather than legal considerations:

- prohibition of sitting in judgement over a foreign executive act,
- danger of imperilling the peace of nations or
- fear of embarrassment of its own executive.

The English courts by judicial restraint and abstention do not want to be involved in difficult and delicate questions as to the motivation of a foreign state. Such a self-imposed restriction by the English courts cannot be altered by their own executive notifying to the courts its indifference or the absence of any embarrassment or of a casus belli (contrary to essential principles of justice and morality). But this judicial limitation then leaves it to its own executive to make any subsequent adjustment or remedy it wishes by diplomatic action.

This foreign act of state doctrine of decided cases does not encompass the day-to-day acts of routine government but mostly property acts of annexation, acquisition, expropriation, and transfer of territory.[8]

There is no principle of public international law that requires states to adopt the act of state doctrine. No state has ever been sued in an international court for failure to apply act of state.

b) U.K. Act of State[9]

The English legal understanding of the rule of law and the equality before the law is tempered by the Royal Prerogative in foreign affairs. Royal Prerogative is a body of customary authority, privilege, and immunity, recognized in common law jurisdictions possessing a monarchy as belonging to the Crown alone. The means by which some of the executive powers of government are possessed are vested in a monarch with regard to the process of governance of his state. It is not subject to parliamentary scrutiny but an individual prerogative can be abolished by legislative enactment.

The Crown enjoys the sole right generally of conducting all foreign affairs. Such matters are entrusted in general to the absolute discretion of the Sovereign, acting through the recognised constitutional channels. In this context, the Crown means the executive or the government. In fact, it is the government which represents its state and determines its policy, though parliament has the right and power to control the executive. It is the state, represented by the government, that conducts foreign affairs, not the judiciary. The courts cannot conduct foreign affairs. They have no power to direct, interfere with or prevent the executive from conducting foreign policy as it deems fit including the treaty-making power. The courts should not be asked to restrain the executive from discretionary decisions such as conclusion and termination of treaties, relations with international organizations, recognizing a state, declaring peace or war, arming and despatching troops. The executive's obligation to provide diplomatic protection to its citizen is – as well – not justiciable.

According to the international relations principle the transactions of independent states between each other are governed by other laws than those which municipal courts administer, such courts have neither the means of deciding what is right nor the power of enforcing any decision which they may make.[10]

While foreign affairs constitute mere facts they may carry legal consequences and set legal rules into operation: for example the recognition of a person as a diplomat will confer immunity from legal process upon him.

The conduct of foreign affairs can in the following cases also constitute public policy:

- If, in a private suit, the Attorney-General brings to the notice of the court a view of the executive on a matter of public policy (ordre public), the court will take direct judicial cognisance of the matter and allow no further evidence on the point.
- In a matter affecting a serious excess of sovereignty by a foreign state the courts are entitled to take account of the declared policy by their executive.
- If courts are called upon to apply or develop a rule of public international law they may consult the executive for guidance as to the principles to be applied. This indeed gives ample room for political expediency.

The main reason for the exercise of judicial discretion is that the courts should in such matters speak with the same voice as the executive in order to avoid a conflict between the courts and the executive. Other reasons could be not to imperil the safety of the state or cause prejudice to the executive's diplomatic relations, or that the topics are considered peculiarly within the province of the executive and outside the experience of the courts.

Foreign affairs can be superseded by legislation (as practised for example in immigration and extradition) and supplanted by an international treaty incorporated into English law by legislation of parliament. But from this submission to the law does not follow that the conduct of foreign relations is subject to judicial review since the subject matter of the prerogative power determines its non-justiciability.

Since the conduct of foreign affairs can be described as facts of state[11] (such as territory, state of war, belligerency, neutrality, civil war or insurgency, diplomatic or consular immunity, existence or abolition of state, government of a recognised state) peculiarly within the cognisance of the executive they can only be proven by a certificate issued from the Foreign Office and cannot be disproved by any other evidence. The reasons are that

- the executive and the judiciary should speak with one voice in matters relating to foreign affairs[12] and
- the judiciary should not embarrass the executive, nor interfere with the conduct of foreign affairs or obstruct their implementation.

Executive guidelines are practised in the following areas of foreign affairs:[13]

- existence of state of war (Crown determines the question whether UK is at war)
- status of foreign states/governments and representatives of states before English courts (state only have locus standi before English courts if the Crown has accepted them as sovereign entities)

- recognition of states/governments with regards to foreign law and validity of foreign acts of state
- territorial extent of the jurisdiction and sovereign rights of the Crown
- extent of the sovereignty of foreign states
- status of military forces.

These international facts are being recognized by the government by official certificate (written statement). Courts have the duty to apply for such a certificate (in the form of an inquiry for judicial notice) which the government has the obligation to supply. The government certificate sets forth its conclusions but does not state the reasons or explain the process of reaching these conclusions.

Though the granting or withholding of the recognition of a fact may differ from other public knowledge the certification by the government is exclusive, conclusive, unquestionable and binding evidence, no evidence is admissible to contradict it. Only if the certificate – after legitimate interpretation by the judiciary – remains vague, ambiguous or temporising can the court make a renewed inquiry to clarify any point of difficulty or doubt or, eventually, can look for other evidence.

In theory, this rule does not apply to facts or events of a historical, geographical, or scientific character; in practice, it is difficult to appreciate the distinction between certifiable recognition and information on factual matters by the government as provable fact which eventually can be challenged and disproved by other means of evidence.

In its certification the government will normally assess the facts and be guided by considerations of international law. But, in cases of political expediency the courts are not allowed to substitute their assessment to that of the executive. The legal effects following the certified fact are a matter solely for the interpretation of the courts. In general, questions of law, whether municipal or international, should be decided by the judiciary, with or without possible guidance by the executive as to the principles.

In recent times, a changing playing field of a new balance of powers could possibly also restrict the future practice of judicial restraint and the Act of State doctrine. The Lord Chancellor in a speech on April 20, 1999 on the Human Rights Act (1998) has said:

> "We have witnessed a shift from what I have termed a "sovereigntist" to a constitutional perception of the role of the judiciary, which emphasized the courts' role as an integral component in constitutional machinery that seeks to secure accountable government."[14]

This tendency of judicial review of government action was recently confirmed by Lord Hoffmann in the "Belmarsh Detainees Case"[15]: The House of Lords had to decide on the existence of an emergency from a threat to the life of the nation by fanatical groups of terrorists. Lord Hoffmann was of the opinion that "terrorist violence, serious as it is, does not threaten our institutions of government or our existence as a civil community" and thus does not justify the suspension of habeas corpus.

References

1 **Halsbury's Laws of England,** (London: Butterworth 1912), p.310

2 **Lord Miller** in: House of Lords, March 24,1999: Regina c/ Bartle and the Commissioner of Police for the Metropolis and others: ex parte Pinochet (2nd Judgement), ILM 1999, vol. 38, p. 58

3 **Lord Berwick** in: House of Lords, November 25, 1998: ex parte Pinochet (1st Judgement), ILM 1998, vol. 37, p. 1302

4 **Brigitte Stern,** Immunités et doctrine de l'Act of State, in: Journal du Droit International, 2006/No.1, p. 63

5 **Lord Nicholls** in: House of Lords, November 25, 1998, ex parte Pinochet (1st Judgement), ILM 1998, vol. 37, p. 1302

6 **Andrea Bianchi,** L'immunité des états et les violations graves des droits de l'homme: la fonction de l'interprète dans la détermination du droit international, in: Revue Générale de Droit International 2004, p. 98

7 **Fritz Alexander Mann,** Foreign Affairs in English Courts, (Oxford: Clarendon Press 1986) p. 180
Prosper Weil, Le contrôle par les tribunaux nationaux de la licéité internationale des actes des états étrangers, in: Annuaire Français de Droit International 1977, p. 9

8 **Michael Singer,** The Act of State doctrine of the United Kingdom: an analysis, with comparisons to United States practice, in: American Journal of International Law, vol. 75, 1981, p. 283 (294)
D.L. Jones, Act of Foreign State in English Law, in: Virginia Journal of International Law, vol. 22 (1982), p. 433

9 For an analysis of cases see:
Fritz Alexander Mann, Foreign Affairs
A.W. Bradley, Judicial protection of the individual against the executive in Great Britain, in: Judicial protection against the executive. National Reports, Max-Planck-Institut für Ausländisches Öffentliches Recht und Völkerrecht (Köln: Carl Heymann Verlag 1969), p. 327
Wilfried Bolewski, Les certificats gouvernementaux relatifs à l'application du droit international public par le juge interne. Étude de la jurisprudence anglaise, in: Revue Générale de Droit International Public, No. 3 1973, p. 672

[10] **Franz Christoph Zeitler,** Judicial review and judicial restraint gegenüber der auswärtigen Gewalt, in: Jahrbuch des Öffentlichen Rechts der Gegenwart, vol. 25 (1976), p. 621
Ernst Petersmann, Act of State doctrine, political question doctrine and gerichtliche Kontrolle der auswärtigen Gewalt, in: Jahrbuch des Öffentlichen Rechts der Gegenwart, vol 25 (1976), p. 587

[11] **Benedetto Conforti,** International law and the role of domestic legal systems (Dordrecht: Martinus Nijhoff Publishers 1993), p. 18

[12] **Lord Atkin** in: The Arantzazu Mendi (1939) A.C. 256 (264(: "Our state cannot speak with two voices on such a matter, the judiciary saying one thing, the executive another."

[13] **Matthias J. Herdegen,** Erklärungen der englischen Krone vor Gerichten in auswärtigen Fragen, in: Zeitschrift für Ausländisches Öffentliches Recht und Völkerrecht, vol. 40 (1980), p. 782

[14] http://www.dca.gov.uk/speeches/1999/20-4-99.htm#5

[15] House of Lords, December 16, 2004, Opinions of the Lords of Appeal for Judgement in the Cause of A (FC) and other (FC) (Appellants) v. Secretary of State for the Home Department (Respondent), ILM vol. 44 (2005), p. 654 ("Belmarsh Detainees Case")

2. Political Question doctrine in the United States of America

a) U.S. Act of Foreign Sate[1]

The traditional U.S. understanding of the common law principle of Act of Foreign State is that a nation is sovereign within its borders, and its domestic actions may not be questioned in the court of another nation. This judicially created doctrine based on the notions of international comity and expediency requires U.S. courts to refrain from sitting in judgment on acts of a governmental character issued by foreign governments within their own territory. The classic definition of this doctrine was spelled out in "Underhill v. Hernandez":[2]

> "Every sovereign state is bound to respect the independence of every other sovereign state, and the courts of one country will not sit in judgment on the acts of the government of another done within its own territory. Redress of grievances by reason of such acts must be obtained through the means open to be availed of by sovereign powers as between themselves."

A defendant may raise the Act of State doctrine as an affirmative defence. A dismissal on Act of State grounds is not a ruling that the court lacks jurisdiction over the case. Not to dismiss on Act of State grounds constitutes a determination that U.S. law should govern the controversy.

The Act of State is recognized in recent cases to be a product of domestic not (customary) international law;[3] it is not a binding rule of American constitutional law but rather an expression of judicial self-restraint:

> "Although originally couched in terms of sovereign immunity, the doctrine as presently developed does not rest on principles of international law or respect for sovereign independence. More recent interpretations of the doctrine instead emphasize the separation of powers rationale – more specifically, the need to preclude judicial encroachment in the field of foreign policy and international diplomacy [...]
>
> In questioning the validity of acts of foreign states, the judiciary may well hinder the Executive's conduct of foreign affairs and the need to

> speak with one voice on the world stage. No such danger is present here and in fact the opposite is true since the Executive's position is amply demonstrated by its decision do indict and prosecute the defendant [...].
>
> In order for the Act of State doctrine to apply, the defendant must establish that his activities are "Acts of State", i.e. that they were taken on behalf of the state and not, as private acts, on behalf of the actor himself. The court fails to see how Noriega's alleged drug trafficking and protection of money launderers could conceivably constitute public action taken on behalf of the Panamanian state."

Contrary to foreign sovereign immunity law which is jurisdictionally-based, the Act of State doctrine is a rule of substantive law not involving jurisdiction. As a judicial policy of restraint its application cannot be waived by a foreign state. Act of State issues only arise when a court must decide – i.e. when the outcome of the case turns upon the effect of official action by a foreign sovereign. Because the doctrine may be invoked by private litigants, it also differs from sovereign immunity, which may be pleaded only by the foreign state itself.

Recently, the Act of State doctrine has found a new justification: The Act is seen as a function of the distribution of federal powers within the constitutional system. The constitution establishes the President – not the courts – as the primary organ of the federal powers in the field of international relations. The Act of State thus counsels the courts not to adjudicate cases that would interfere with the executive branch's handling of foreign affairs. The doctrine is said to have constitutional underpinnings that arise out of the basic relationships between the branches of government in a system of separation of powers.

> "The Act of State doctrine once rested on the inherent nature of sovereign authority and principles of international law. Now, in this country at least, the doctrine's foundation has shifted to the interest in preserving the separation of powers between the branches of government (Banco Nacional de Cuba v. Sabbatino, 376 U.S. 398, 423, 84, S.Ct. 923,937, 11 L.Ed.´2d 804 (1964)). A court declines to exercise jurisdiction over a case that may hinder or embarrass the executive in the conduct of foreign affairs in deference to the proper distribution of functions between the judicial and the political branches in the area of international relations."[4]

Judicial adjucation may embarrass the executive branch before the international community. Particularly acute should the court adjudicate a dispute which is simultaneously being handled by the State Department and the court if it comes to a decision that is inconsistent with that of the Department. This would seriously frustrate the unity of design.

Another precision to the U.S. Act of State doctrine has been added in the field of clear and serious violation of international law (international law exception): With international fundamental human rights and ius cogens, additional acts have come under special international scrutiny:

> "In the twentieth century the international community has come to recognize the common danger posed by the flagrant disregard of basic human rights and particularly the right to be free of torture [...]. In the modern age, humanitarian and practical considerations have combined to lead the nations of the world to recognize that respect for the fundamental human rights is in their individual and collective interest. Among the rights universally proclaimed by all nations [...] is the right to be free of physical torture. Indeed, for the purposes of civil liability, the torturer has become – like the pirate and slave trader before him – hostis humani generis, an enemy of mankind."[5]

This erosion of the Act of State doctrine is the result of greater democratization and awareness of rights of citizens over rulers.[6]

The typical act of state (property expropriation by a foreign sovereign) would adversely affect many plaintiffs. The courts have taken notice that the executive branch has better access to resources superior to those of the courts in making and enforcing decisions which determine the liabilities of foreign governments. A piecemeal litigation of the court, on the other hand, would be less likely to protect the rights of all the potential plaintiffs than would a resolution of the matter en masse through diplomatic channels. U.S. courts will not shield foreign sovereign acts under Act of State when that state's actions is not in accord with U.S. policy and adversely affects property and rights within the U.S.

The U.S. Act of State doctrine covers principally the following four controversial situations:

- nationalisation or expropriation,
- the situs of debts and public loans,
- a commercial act exception (when sovereign immunity overlaps with the Act of State doctrine) and
- non-expropriation context (conspiracy and slander actions)[7]

Apart from the public policy exception the Act of State is generally excluded in cases wherein the State Department provides the courts with an executive declaration stating that it has no objections to a case involving a foreign act being litigated.[8] It is the recognition of the primacy of the executive in the conduct of foreign affairs that led the Supreme Court to hold the act of state doctrine inapplicable where the President has so advised.[9] Even though the executive is charged with the primary responsibility to conduct foreign affairs, the court should not abstain from performing its traditional adjudicatory function when the executive has assured that doing so would be consistent with American foreign policy.[10]

b) U.S. Political Question doctrine in foreign affairs

According to the U.S. Supreme Court conduct of foreign relations is committed by the constitution to the executive and legislative – the "political" departments of the government, and the propriety of what may be done in the exercise of this political power is not subject to judicial inquiry or decision.[11] In U.S. law, a ruling that something is a political question is a statement by a federal court, declining to rule in cases because

- the constitution has committed decision-making on this subject to another branch of federal government,
- there are inadequate standards for the court to apply or
- the court feels it is prudent not to interfere.

An interesting historical argument about the influence of the traditional deference of British courts in relation to foreign affairs on American jurisprudence is provided by Thomas M. Franck:[12]

> "What we have here is some sort of Faustian pact between the courts and the political organs. The use of British case law (UK Act of State doctrine) to plant the political question doctrine on American soil may be seen as an expedient by a fragile federal judiciary bent first on establishing its supremacy in domestic matters and thus looking for a convenient, relatively inexpensive "giveback" to throw to the political branches and the states."

The major purpose for the U.S. doctrine in legal practice has been the prevention of judicial interference in the presidential conduct of foreign relations. The courts feel obliged to support the presidential conduct of foreign affairs as fully and completely as possible. The state through its chief executive is vested with all the powers of government necessary to maintain an effective control of international relations. The president as the sole organ is constitutionally charged with primary responsibility for external relations, he is the key actor in foreign affairs. In the vast external realm, with its important, complicated, delicate and manifold problems, the president alone has the power to speak or listen as a representative of the nation.[13] He has his confidential sources of information. He has his agents in the form of diplomatic, consular and other officials. Secrecy in respect of information gathered by them may be highly necessary, and the premature disclosure of it productive of harmful results.

The U.S constitution contains no textual basis for excluding, limiting or altering the role and authority of the courts when they are called upon to decide cases which relate to U.S. foreign relations. Within the separation of powers the courts have no authority to conduct U.S. foreign relations. U.S. courts apply the political question doctrine to ensure the proper distribution of functions between the judicial and political branches of government on matters bearing on foreign affairs. This doctrine bars the courts from resolving cases that raise issues more appropriately committed to the discretion of other branches of government.

Out of this basic relationship between the branches of government in a system of separation of powers pragmatic concerns about the effective execution of U.S. foreign policy appear to demand that the executive branch of the government be accorded a salient role when such matters are involved and courts have used judicial deference and abstention in such cases.

The classic catalogue of conditions to which the Political Question doctrine applies was set forth by the U.S. Supreme Court:[14] some are prudential; others are rooted in the separation of powers:

- textual commitment of the issue to a "coordinate political department",
- lack of judicially discoverable or manageable standards to resolve the issue
- the impossibility of deciding the issue without making a nonjudicial policy determination
- the potential for showing a lack of respect that is otherwise due other branches of government
- an "unusual need for unquestioning adherence to a political decision already made", or
- the potential for embarrassment from "multifarious pronouncements by various departments on one question".

The court also mentioned the inappropriateness for the judiciary to throw itself into the "political thicket" of foreign affairs. It observed that not only does resolution of such issues frequently turn on standards that defy judicial application, or involve the exercise of a discretion demonstrably committed to the executive, but many such questions uniquely demand single-voiced statement of the government's views.

A variety of reasons and consideration for deference or abstention by the judiciary have been advanced in support of the Political Question doctrine. They basically centre on the understanding of international law (a.) and the political assessment of the constitutional framework (b.)[15]

a) International law

Under the impression that international law is unenforceable and rarely respected by states U.S. courts have the tendency to treat international law differently and more politically than they do other law. The international legal system – especially customary international law to which the U.S. can only be one contributor among many – is seen to be biased against U.S. interests. Therefore, the courts often prefer guidance from the executive branch in these matters.

Their judicial deference is also due to the fact that they consider to be unfamiliar with the international law and to lack access to all necessary – especially sensitive or confidential – facts (judicial fact-finding incapacities).

According to the Chief Justice of the Supreme Court of Texas, Thomas R. Philips[16], the influence of international law will be growing in areas falling under state court jurisdiction due to new conventions. Already state courts are probably handling more international law cases than do federal courts. But also the international law-related caseload of U.S. federal courts will be increasing because international law's concerns have shifted from relations among states to relationship between states and their citizens. The internationnal human rights regime challenges states to reexamine the justifiability of their practices. The Supreme Court has reason to examine international human rights norms and decisions interpreting them for the normative and functional insights.[17] Normative comparisons with human rights law may therefore prove fruitful.

Recently, the Supreme Court in "Hamdan v. Rumsfeld"[18] has reserved the right to interpret (customary and treaty) international law (such as the Geneva Conventions).

b) Political assessment of the constitutional framework

For reasons of state in international affairs and the judiciary's understanding of the separation of powers the courts want to maintain and protect the U.S., its policies and interests. Out of fear that court decisions might have important and indeterminate international effects detrimental to the U.S the courts refrain from multifarious pronouncements. On the ground of expediency it is also argued that court decisions may frustrate U.S. efforts to present a unified position to the international community on international matters (one-voice-policy). On the other hand, court judgements might undermine the government's need for flexibility in international affairs.

Some matters of non-justiciability in the field of foreign affairs can be found in the following cases:

- establishing legitimacy of a revolutionary regime in Mexico[19],
- recognition of states, diplomatic status or termination of treaties by the President.[20] Article II, section 2 clause 2 of the Constitution states that the President has the power to make treaties, provided that two-thirds of the Senate concur. However, the Constitution does not explicitly address the question of how a treaty may be abrogated. The court held that the basic question is political and therefore nonjustiable because it involves the authority of the President in the conduct of foreign relations and the extent to which the Senate or the Congress is authorized to negate the action of the President,
- application for an injunction restraining the U.S. from dealing with South Africa in pursuance of UN Security Council Resolution[21],
- illegality of military and economic assistance by the U.S. to Israel[22] or San Salvador[23],
- challenges to presidential war-making.[24] The resolution of the question whether the President's deployment of troops violated the war powers resolution and various provisions of the Constitution would require the judicial branch to intrude impermissibly into the realm of executive and legislative authority. The judicial branch is neither equipped nor empowered to intrude into the realm of foreign affairs where the Constitution grants operational powers only to the two political branches and where decisions are made based on political and policy considerations.[25]

While such deference (self-restraint or self-limitation) was once extensive, at a time when international relations were considered the exclusive province of diplomacy, it seems to be diminishing at a steady pace.[26]

References

1 **Michael C. Davis,** Domestic development of international law: A proposal for an international concept of the Act of State doctrine, in: Texas International Law Journal, vol. 20, no. 1 (1985), p.341

2 (1897) 168 U.S. 250

3 United States v. Noriega, Case No. 88-79-CR, U.S.District Court for the Southern District of Florida, June 8, 1980, ILR 99,145

4 Williams v. Curtiss-Wright Corporation, U.S.Court of Appeals, Third Circuit, November 29, 1982, ILR 81, 516

5 Filartiga v. Pena-Irala, 630 F. 2nd 876 (2nd Circuit 1980).
Andrea Bianchi, The Act of State: The state of the act. Judicial interpretation and human rights enforcement, in: **Marcelo G. Kohen,** Promoting justice, human rights

and conflict resolution through international law. Liber Amicorum Lucius Caflisch, (Leiden: Martinus Nijhoff Publishers 2007), p. 129 (142)

6 **James Biser Whisker,** The supremacy of the state in international law. The Act of State doctrine, (Lewiston: Edwin Mellen Press 2003) p. 4

7 **Ernest K. Bankas,** The state immunity, p. 243

8 Bernstein v. N.V. Nederlandische-Amerikaansche Stoomvaart Maatschappi, 21 F.2nd 375 (2nd Circuit, 1954)

9 First National City Bank v. Banco Nacional de Cuba, 406 U.S. 759 (1972)

10 **Sandra Day O'Connor,** Federalism of free nations, in: **Thomas M. Franck/Gregory H. Fox (ed.),** International law decisions in national courts (New York: Transnational Publishers 1996), p. 13

11 Oetjen v. Central Leather Co., 246 U.S. 297 (1918)

12 **Thomas M. Franck,** Political questions – judicial answers: Does the rule of law apply to foreign affairs? (Princeton: Princeton University Press 1992), p. 12

13 United States v. Curtiss-Wright Export Corporation, 299 U.S. 304 (1936)

14 Baker v. Carr, 369 U.S. 186 (1962)

15 **Jonathan I. Charney,** Judicial deference in foreign relation, in: American Journal of International Law, vol. 83 (1989), p. 805
Michael J. Glennon, Foreign affairs and the Polical Question doctrine, in: American Journal of International Law, vol. 83 (1989), p. 814

16 **Thomas R. Philips,** State Supreme Courts: Local Courts in a global world, in: Texas International Law Journal, vol. 38 (2003), p. 557

17 **Gerald L. Neumann,** The uses of International Law in constitutional interpretation, in: American Journal of International Law, vol. 98 (2004) p. 82 (87)

18 Hamdan v. Rumsfeld, Supreme Court June 29, 2006, in: ILM vol. 45 (2006), p. 1130

19 Oetjen v. Central Leather Co, 246 U.S. 297 (1918)

20 Goldwater v. Carter, 444 U.S. 996 (1979)

21 Diggs v. Richardson, 555 F. 2d 848 (1976)

22 Dickson v. Ford, 521 F. 2d 234 (1975)

23 Crocket v. Reagan, 720 F. 2d 1355 (1983)

24 Holtzmann v. Schlesinger, 484 F. 2d 1307 (1973) – Vietnam
Conyers v. Reagan, 578 F. Supp. 324 (D.D.C. 1984) – Grenada
Crockett v. Reagan, 558 F. Supp. 893 (D.D.C. 1982) – El Salvador
Dellums v. Bush, 752 F. Supp. 1141 (D.D.C. 1990) – Persian Gulf
John Doe et al. v. George W. Bush, President/Donald H. Rumsfeld, Secretary of Defense, U.S. Court of Appeals for the First Circuit, 323 F.3d 133 (2003) – Iraq
See **Edward B. Firmage,** War powers and Political Questions, in: Columbia Law Review, vol. 49 (1977) p. 65
Gregory H. Fox, Reexamining the Act of State doctrine: An integrated conflicts analysis, in: Harvard International Law Journal, vol. 33 (1992), p.521

Wayne McCormack, The Political Question doctrine- jurisprudentially, in: University of Detroit Mercy Law Review, vol. 70, no. 4 (1993) p.793
Louis Henkin, Is there a "Political Question" doctrine?, in: The Yale Law Journal, vol. 85, no. 5 (1976), p.597

[25] Ange v. Bush, 752 Fed. Suppl. (D.D.C. 1990) 309 (District Court, District of Columbia

[26] **Benedetto Conforti,** International law and the role of domestic legal systems, (Dordrecht: Martinus Nijhoff Publishers 1993), p. 17

[27] **Sandra Day O'Connor,** Federalism of free nations, in: **Thomas M. Franck/Gregory H. Fox (ed.),** International law decisions in national courts, p. 13

3. French Act of Government

a) Government of judges

The French legal system still today carries the imprint of the Revolution, which clearly subordinated the legal branch to political power. This historical aversion to a strong judiciary reflects a fundamental aspect of French social as well as legal culture. What originated in the royal absolutism to keep the judiciary subordinate continues today as a perceived threat to the absolute legislative and executive powers as well as the French definition of "raison d'Etat". This is at the very core of the French approach to statehood and the separation of powers. Differently from the U.S. or Germany, France today still feels very strongly about this political separation of powers, which basically differs from the idea of checks and balances.

In 1921, Edouard Lambert's study of American judicial politics[1] coined the phrase of "government of judges" denoting an unconstrained system of judicial review. This has become an international catch-phrase. Lambert focused on the socialization and ideological orientation of judges and examined the social impact of judicial decisions. He pointed to the possible danger that the judiciary could control the economic, social, and political evolution. His fear of a general judicialization of the policy-making processes in French society or a politicization of justice through judicial activism was at first meant to protect legislative actions, later it was also extended by others to executive decisions especially in the conduct of foreign affairs. The fear of the "rule of judges" (juristocracy) entailing a "government by the judiciary" became the basis of a central French legal concept.[2]

3) Act of Government (acte de gouvernement)

The French Constitution of the Fifth Republic (1958, Articles 5 II, 13, 14, 52) has two objectives with reference to foreign affairs:

- to preserve the freedom of action for the executive and
- to uphold the prerogative of the President in the field of foreign policy ("domaine réservé")

On the other hand, the French judiciary itself (be it administrative or constitutional) practises a judicial restraint in international relations of their government. Its doctrine of "Act of Government" (or: prerogative act) is not based on any legislative text but developed through jurisprudence.

The Act of Government is not considered as an administrative act, as it is the expression of political duties and not of administrative duties, carried out by executive bodies. Among these governmental competences and responsibilities are diplomatic duties which express the international activities of the state. Due to what could be called an irreducibility of the political to the juridical, these duties are fundamentally indeterminable: they cannot be defined by the rule of law. Consequently, the Act taken to carry out these duties cannot be the objective of an application of a standard; it can only be a pure decision of last resort: a sovereign decision. Such a decision may thus appear non-justiciable by its nature, since its eventual submission to a jurisdictional control could only lead to the judge rendering a decision of similar nature, substituting his (political) decision to that of the executive. Consequently, it appears that in French legal understanding it is due to its nature that a government's action in foreign affairs escapes any jurisdictional control.[3]

The most striking examples and core cases of Act of Government in foreign affairs are the executive decisions in the conduct of war and international relations:

The petition of Greenpeace France against the restarting of a series of nuclear tests in French Polynesia in 1995 was rejected by the Conseil d'Etat[4] (the oldest French court, but one which is not mentioned in any Constitution) on the following grounds;

- the President's decision cannot be detached from the conduct of the international relations of France and consequently falls outside any control by the courts and
- the administrative court is, in these circumstances, incompetent to hear the petition of Greenpeace France claiming that this decision be quashed for "ultra vires" ("excès de pouvoir").

In an earlier judgement the Conseil d'Etat[5] stated:

> "The Presidential decree of 4 July 1973 which is being challenged created, around the Atoll of Mururoa, a security zone extending for 60 nautical miles contiguous to the territorial sea (for atmospheric nuclear tests in French Polynesia.). The decision which is being challenged suspended maritime navigation within this zone. Both of these decisions relate to the international relations of the French state. It follows that

these decisions are not within the competence of administrative tribunals."

Other cases concerned peacetime diplomatic undertakings of the executive in the conduct of foreign affairs;

In 1974 French naval authorities destroyed a foreign shipwrecked cargo vessel 22 miles outside French territorial waters on the high seas because it constituted a danger to the safety of both the French coast and French territorial waters and to the safety in those waters. By reason of the dangerous character of the cargo made up of explosives and dynamite no other measure was considered sufficient to remove the danger. In these circumstances the Conseil d'Etat[6] held that the destruction of the wreck did not violate any principle of international law and did not constitute fault capable of engaging the responsibility of the State for damages.

Claims against alleged failures of France at the time of negotiation of the Evian Agreement in 1962 which led to the expropriation of property of French nationals by Algerian authorities following the independence of Algeria were considered "inadmissible" by the Conseil d'Etat.[7]

In another case the Conseil d'Etat[8] examined whether measures taken by France for the diplomatic protection of its nationals in Egypt were so inadequate as to engage its responsibility. It held that the extension of diplomatic protection comes within the discretionality of the executive, for reasons simply of domestic order.[9] It also ruled that the French state cannot be made responsible for damages in its capacity as signatory of an international agreement,[10] for alleged negligence in negotiations[11] or insufficiency of the provision of such an agreement, nor for failure of the French state to publish such an agreement, since all this involved the relations of France with foreign states.

The interpretation of international treaties by the French judiciary is subject to differentiation according to the independence of the different judicial branches:

Article 54 of the Constitution declares the Constitutional Court competent for the examination of international engagements. The Constitutional Court has declared itself authorized to review the legal commitments taken in application of the constituent international treaties.

Traditionally, the Conseil d'Etat recognized the competence of the executive in matters concerning the interpretation of treaties: It was not for the Conseil d'Etat to decide on the application of an instrument touching the relations of France with a foreign power.[12] With regard to the interpretation of treaties a discontinuance of jurisprudence and an important step and elegant shift in the direction of the independence of the courts with respect to the executive was made with a judgement of the Conseil d'Etat in 1990:[13]

Instead of making a reference to the Ministry of Foreign Affairs for an interpretation of treaty provisions, as required by previous jurisprudence, the Conseil d'Etat adopted the position that it could establish the meaning of an international treaty provision without such a reference.

Due to the increasing internationalization of French administrative law a new category of administrative foreign acts ("acte détachable des relations internationales qui ne gêne pas la liberté de manoeuvre gouvernementale")[14] is emerging in regional courts but also in the Conseil d'Etat in which the judiciary feels free to proceed independently from the practice of government certificate. They apply to situations and decisions where the executive is less bound by constitutional obligations. Two groups of governmental decisions can be distinguished:

- Acts of foreign administration (ascertainment of diplomatic status, extension of territory, application of laws or immunity from jurisdiction of a non-recognized state, extradition matters) and
- Acts in execution of treaties.

The Cour de Cassation in 1992[15] held:

The conclusion of contracts for the sale of war materials by a commercial undertaking was separable from both the Executive decision of authorization or agreement to which it was subject and the conduct of the relations of the French Government with the authorities of foreign states. Consequently the conclusion of the contract at issue did not constitute an "acte de gouvernement".

This new category of cases significantly diminishes the area of application of the "Act of Government" doctrine in foreign affairs and seems thus to pierce the veil of the national order, fully embrace the international order and principally advance the rule of law.

References

1 **Edouard Lambert,** Le gouvernement des juges et la lutte contre la législation sociale aux Etats-Unis – l'expérience américaine du contrôle judiciaire de la constitutionalité des lois, (Paris: Girard 1921)
For a contemporary interpretation see:
Séverine Brondel/Norbert Foulquier/Luc Henschling (ed.), Gouvernement des juges et démocratie, (Paris: Publications de la Sorbonne 2001)

[2] For the historical developments in French legal history and culture see:
Michael H. Davis, A government of judges: An historical re-view, in: The American Journal of Comparative Law, vol. 35 (1987) p. 559
Alec Stone, The birth of judicial politics in France. The Constitutional Council in comparative perspective, (New York/Oxford: Oxford University Press 1992)

[3] **Pierre Serrand,** L'acte de gouvernement. Contribution à la théorie des fonctions juridiques de l'État, Thèse Paris II 1996
Elisabeth Zoller, Droit des relations extérieures, (Paris: Presses Universitaires de France 1992), p.300

[4] CE, 29 September 1995, Case Association Greenpeace France, translated by Institute of Global Law, University College London, http://www.ucl.ac.uk/laws/global_/french-cases/etat/print_etat.shtm/?29sept1995

[5] CE, 11 July 1975, Paris de Ballardière and Others, in: International Law Reports, vol. 74 (1987), p. 95

[6] CE, 23 October 1987, Nachfolger Navigation Company Ltd. And Others, in: International Law Reports, vol. 80 (1989) p. 3

[7] CE, 29 November 1968, Tallagrand, in: International Law Reports, vol. 72 (1987) p. 218

[8] CE, 18 December 1968, Beinisch, in: International Law Reports, vol. 72 (1987) p. 221

[9] CE, 25 March 1988, Société Sapvin, in: International Law Reports, vol. 89 (1992) p. 6

[10] CE, 13 July 1961, In re Société Indochinoise d'Électricité, in: International Law Reports, vol. 42 (1971) p. 8

[11] CE, 29 October 1954, In re Taurin and Mérienne, in: International Law Reports, year 1954 (1957) p. 15

[12] CE, 28 May 1937, Decerf's Case, in: Annual Digest and Reports of Public International Law Cases, years 1935-1937 (1941) p. 347

[13] CE, 29 June 1990, G.I.S.T.I., in: International Law Reports, vol. 111 (1998) p. 499
CE, 18 December 1999, Case SARL du parc d'activités de Blotzheim et SCI Haselaecker, in: Revue française de droit administratif 1999, p. 331
Hélène Tourard, p. 322
M.F. Buffet-Tchaskaloff, L'interprétation des traités internationaux par le Conseil d'État, in: Revue générale de droit international public 1991, p. 109.
For recent decisions see:
Jörg Gundel, Der Status des Völkerrechts in der französischen Rechtsordnung nach der neueren Rechtssprechung des Conseil d'Etat: Von der Öffnung zum Rückzug?, in: Archiv des Völkerrechts, vol. 37 (1999), p. 438

[14] **Frédérique Rueda,** p. 213
Pierre Serrand, p. 338
Olivier Cayla, Le contrôle des mesures d'exécution des traités: réduction ou négation de la théorie des actes de gouvernement, in: Revue française de droit administratif 1994, p. 1
Jacques Moreau, Internationalisation du droit administratif français et déclin de

l'acte de gouvernement, in: Mélanges en l'honneur de Yvon Loussouarn, (Paris: Dalloz 1994), p. 293

[15] 30 June 1992, SA Dassault v. Assoc. Européenne, in: International Law Reports, vol. 196 (1997), p. 216
Olivier Cayla, p. 1

4. Judicial review of foreign affairs in Germany

The German Basic Law provides for a traditional and strict separation of powers. The executive is bound by legislation and the law, article 20 para. 3 (principle of the rule of law – "Rechtsstaatsprinzip"). By virtue of this article, all German State organs are bound by international law norms applicable in Germany. Article 25 not only affirms the supremacy of international law and gives clear precedence to international law over domestic law, but also provides for the direct application of relevant international norms to claims by individual citizens. Judging from the increasing number of opinions concerning article 25 issued by the Federal Constitutional Court, customary international law is playing an increasingly important role in the German legal system.

All state organs are, in particular, obliged to refrain from any measure which would give effect, in the sphere of application of the Basic Law, to acts of other States which violate general principles of international law; moreover, they must also refrain from any measure which would contribute – in a decisive way – to violations of such general principles by acts of other States. If this obligation conflicts with the constitutional obligation to cooperate with other States and other subjects of international law a solution must be found which is based upon a fair balance between these obligations. This qualification does not apply, however, with respect to international law norms having the rank of ius cogens (serious breach of human rights generally recognized by the international community – cases of heinous crimes) from which no State may deviate unilaterally or by means of treaty law. Acts of foreign States which violate such norms must not be recognized as legal and German authorities must not contribute to such acts.[1]

The Federal President represents the Federation ("Bund") in international affairs, article 59 para. 1. The conduct of foreign affairs is within the competence and responsibility of the Federation, article 32 para. 1. The primacy of the conduct of foreign affairs lies with the (federal) executive. In principle, acts of foreign policy not covered by article 59 para. 1 (political treaties) are matters to be decided solely by the (federal) government.[2] According to the general principle of separation of powers, foreign policy forms part of the government's function and prerogative. The federal government alone is responsible for preliminary treaty discussions and, subsequently, only the government has the power to decide whether or not to ratify a treaty and, if necessary to repeal or to extend it. Such an act in accordance with article 59 para.2 Basic Law is a non-justiciable executive act in the area of foreign powers, and cannot be challenged by constitutional complaint.[3]

Several articles of the Basic Law (1 para.2, 9 para 2, 23, 24, 26, 87a, 115a) deal with the substance of international cooperation of Germany. These articles may even prime over the individual human rights as guaranteed by the Basic Law.[4]

Under the rule of law ("Rechtsstaat"), all public authority is subject to judicial review, article 19 para. 4 Basic Law. German constitutional law neither requires nor precludes judicial self-restraint in foreign relations. There is no "political question" doctrine as such in German constitutional law; everything is adjudicable including the highly politicized field of foreign affairs.[5] Even though separation of powers constitutes the basic organizing principle of German constitutional law there is no abstention by the judiciary from political questions. The German Constitutional Court as the final interpreter of German constitutional law watches over the application of all constitutional principles.

In the independent interpretation of the Basic Law the Constitutional Court is free to determine in its jurisprudence whether and how it controls the conduct of foreign affairs by the executive. Over the years it has developed a coherent theory applicable to the adjudication of foreign affairs cases. In 1955 the Court said about the constitutionality of the "Saar Statute"[6]:

> "The Federal Constitutional Court, when it has to measure an international treaty which regulates the political relations of the Federation (article 59 para. 2 Basic Law) against the Basic Law, must not lose sight of the political position from which the treaty has arisen, of the political realities it seeks to shape or to alter [....]
>
> As long as this basic tendency towards constitutionality is maintained, as regards the choice of individual measures provided for in the treaty, the treaty-making organs of the Federal Republic of Germany must have broad scope for political discretion, especially since the gamut of treaty solutions open to choice is in practice restricted to what is politically attainable vis-à-vis the given contracting party [...]
>
> A legal finding of unconstitutionality is excluded in principle by the fact that the situation created by the treaty is "closer to the Basic Law" than the previously existing one. If only a treaty arrangement in full accord with the Basic Law were to be counted as constitutional, that

> would mean advocating a constitutional rigorism which could be encapsulated in the following sentence: the bad may not give way to the better, because the best (or from this viewpoint, the sole good) is not attainable. This cannot be desired by the Basic Law."

In this early decision the German Constitutional Court gives an interesting definition of the role of the judicial branch in international negotiations and the leeway extended to the executive. First of all, any legal analysis of international negotiations will have to consider the influence of the national legal order and the scope of judicial review. The German judiciary has realized that the terms of an international agreement are not under the sole responsibility of a national government, but result from intensive bargaining with other actors that are not subject to German legal constraints. The outcome of such negotiations cannot be expected to conform totally to the German position. Consequently, the Court has developed the theory of approximation as margin of legal appreciation. The government may conclude an international agreement that does not conform to constitutional requirements if the situation created by the agreement is at least closer to the constitution than before. Furthermore, the Court has accepted the realities of international relations by giving a wide margin of appreciation to the executive in its determinations and prognoses in foreign affairs.[7] The executive is supposed to command the necessary knowledge and therefore carries the political responsibility in foreign affairs.

In the case "East-West Basic Treaty"[8] it defined the role of law ("Rechtsstaat") and the principle of judicial self-restraint:

> "Among the interpretive principles important particularly in connection with the constitutional review of treaties is also that in interpreting constitutional provisions relating to the Federal Republic's relationships with other States, their demarcatory character, that is the room for manoeuvre they allow in policy making, ought not to be left out of account. In this demarcation the Basic Law sets legal limits to every political power, in the area of foreign policy too; this is the essence of the rule of law constituted by the Basic Law. The implementation of this constitutional order is incumbent ultimately on the Federal Constitutional Court.
>
> The principle of judicial self-restraint that the Federal Constitutional Court imposes on itself does not mean a curtailment or weakening of its powers as just set out, but refraining from "playing politics" that is, intervening in the area of free policy making set up and demarcated by the Constitution. It accordingly aims at keeping the leeway for free policy making guaranteed by the Constitution for the other constitutional organs open."

In 1980 the Constitutional Court decided on the government's discretion in granting protection against foreign states ("Hess Case")[9]:

> "The Federal Government is due broad discretion in respect of the question whether and in what way it guaranties protection against foreign countries, and that the administrative courts have consequently confined themselves to testing the Federal Government's acts and omissions for errors of discretion. This view is in line with the Federal Constitutional Court's case law according to which particularly in the foreign policy sphere, the Federal Government, like all other State organs called on for political action, is in general granted broad room for political discretion [....]
>
> The breadth of the discretion in the foreign sphere has its basis in the fact that the shaping of foreign relations and occurrences cannot be determined by the will of the Federal Republic of Germany alone, but is in many ways dependent on circumstances beyond its determination. In order to make it possible to secure the various political objectives of the Federal Republic of Germany in the context of what is permissible constitutionally and in international law, the Basic Law grants the organs of foreign power very broad room for manoeuvre in their assessment of situations of foreign-policy relevance, like the expediency of possible action [...]
>
> It must be left to its foreign-policy assessment and evaluation how far it regards other measures as appropriate and [....] as advisable. [...] Having regard to the broad discretion allowed it, there can be no constitutional objections to the Federal Government regarding as inadvisable the approaches to the United Nations Organization....Its assessment that such steps would not promise success cannot –particularly taking the attitude of the United Nations themselves into account – be regarded as a failure of discretion [...]
>
> In view of this state of affairs, it is of essential importance for the upholding of the interests of the Federal Republic of Germany that it appears at international level with a single voice, upheld by the competent organs of external power [...] Great reticence is incumbent on the courts in assessing any legal views of those organs that may be wrongful in international law as failures of discretion. This ought to be taken into account at most where adoption of the legal view in question constituted arbitrariness towards a citizen, and could therefore no longer be understood from any reasonable viewpoint, even in foreign-policy terms [...]

> It is not a matter of the courts to put their assessment of possible effects of such steps at international level in the place of the assessments by the organs of external power. That the Federal Government's assessment can no longer on any rational view be seen as reasonable, even having regard to the objects of constitutional protection of the complainant that are at stake, cannot be established [...]"

In the "Pershing II and Cruise Missile Case"[10] the Court entered again the political thicket of foreign affairs and gave the following guidelines of legal standards for its assessment:

> "Assessments and evaluation of a foreign-policy or defence-policy nature are up to the Federal Government. The Basic Law sets only the bound of obvious arbitrariness to the power of judgment that is accordingly due the Federal Government. Within this extreme limit, the Federal Constitutional Court does not have to review whether evaluations or assessments of the Federal government are right or wrong, since legal criteria for this are not present; they have to be taken responsibility for politically [...]
>
> The allocation in principle of acts in international transaction to the area of competence of the executive is based on the assumption that institutionally and in the long term it would be typically only the government that will adequately dispose of the personal, material and organizational capacities to respond speedily and properly to changing external positions and thus carry out in the best possible way the national task of responsibly handling foreign affairs.
>
> There is therefore by no means a deficit of democracy if the executive has even exclusive powers for far-reaching and perhaps existential decisions in the area of foreign affairs. Accordingly, political risks that may possibly be bound up with this separation of powers have therefore, according to the Constitution, to be put up with."

The Court's limitation of the political assessment in foreign affairs was emphasized in the "GDR-Citizenship Case":[11]

> "The assessment in international law of Germany's legal position by the competent State organs of the Federal Republic of Germany could be opposed by the Federal Constitutional Court only were it plainly against (manifestly contrary to) international law. This cannot be the case here [...]"

The fact that the Court reached the merits of a case so clearly within the political sphere attests to the German courts' emphatic rejection of the political question doctrine.[12]

The matter was further clarified in the "Chemical Weapons Storage Case"[13]:

> "This broad freedom of action can be reviewed by the courts only to a limited extent, depending on the specific nature of the area at issue, the possibilities of arriving subject at an adequately certain judgement and the importance of the objects of legal protection at stake [...]
>
> It is only in very special circumstances that this freedom of action can be restricted because only a particular measure can meet the protective obligation [....] The complainant must conclusively show that the public authorities have either not taken protective measures at all or that manifestly the regulations and measures adopted are entirely unsuitable or completely inadequate to secure the object of protection."

In 1994 the Court[14] decided a most pressing issue in the political debate: It ruled that the three "out of area" deployments of German Armed Forces in UN peace-keeping and peace-enforcing operation (in the Adriatic, Bosnia-Herzegovina and Somalia) were covered by the authorization in Article 24 para. 2 of the Basic Law to join a "system of collective security".

In a criminal case involving diplomatic immunity ("Tabatabai Case")[15] the Federal Supreme Court of Justice dealt with the question whether operative acts of the executive, in particular the Foreign Office, in matters of foreign affairs are binding upon the courts and thus cannot be reviewed. It took the position that it was not bound by the legal view of the Foreign Office which established the immunity of the accused and decided against it. Regardless of the competence of the Foreign Office to shape the relations of the Federal Republic of Germany with foreign countries the court felt obliged to examine, within its own competence, whether immunity has been established in a specific case according to section 20 of the Act on the Constitution of the Courts.

The attitude of German Constitutional Court in the field of judicial review of foreign affairs can be summed up as follows:

It created rules governing the weight and probity of government evidence in foreign affairs litigation. Even while asserting its unlimited right of review, it developed the evidentiary presumption of constitutionality and international legality in favour of the government's use of its discretion to choose to pursue one among several courses of action and prediction of future effects and developments which can be challenged only on the ground of bad faith or arbitrariness.

The Court recognized a core body of state conduct, the government's core legal competence[16] and political responsibility in foreign affairs to which the only criteria (rational standard) for legal assessment and control is that of obvious arbitrariness.[17]

This practice allows the government substantial latitude in carrying out its foreign policy, while at the same time preserving individuals' ability to challenge the lawfulness of government actions.[18] While proceeding under a strong presumption that the governmental action in foreign affairs is valid, German courts do not bar themselves from hearing cases with foreign policy implications. This jurisprudence consonant with the rule of law has developed salutary effects on the legal culture of a society where the last word of interpretation of the law lies with the judiciary.[19]

References

[1] **Rainer Hofmann,** The German Federal Constitutional Court and Public International Law: New decisions, new approaches?, in: German Yearbook of International Law vol. 47 (2004), p. 9
Stephen Hobe/Christian Tietje, Government criminality: The judgment of the German Federal Constitutional Court of 24 October 1996, in: German Yearbook of International Law vol. 39 (1996) p. 523

[2] Bundesverfassungsgericht, 12 July 1994, in: International Law Reports, vol. 106 (1997), p. 320 (335) – International military operations – Somalia

[3] 21 March 1957, in: Decisions of the Federal Constitutional Court- Federal Republic of Germany, (Baden-Baden: Nomos 1992), vol. 1, p. 92 (94)

[4] **Rüdiger Wolfrum,** Auswärtige Beziehungen und Verteidigungspolitik, in: **Peter Badura/Horst Dreier,** Festschrift 50 Jahre Bundesverfassungsgericht, (Tübingen: Mohr Siebeck 2000) Vol. 2, p. 693 (716)

[5] **Rudolf Geiger,** Grundgesetz und Völkerrecht, (München: C.H. Beck 1994) 2nd ed., p. 147

[6] 4 May 1955, in: Decisions vol. 1, p. 70 (77),
see also 18 April 1996 (Land reform II case), in: Decisions vol. 3 (2005), p.54 (63)

[7] **Uwe Kischel,** The State as a non-unitary actor: The role of the judicial branch in international negotiations, in: Archiv des Völkerrechts vol. 39 (2001), p.268

[8] 31 July 1973, in: Decisions vol. 1, p. 244 (254)

[9] 16 December 1980, in: Decisions vol. 2, p. 391

[10] 18 December 1984, in: Decisions vol. 2, p.511

[11] 21 October 1987, in: Decisions vol. 2, p.718

[12] **George Slyz,** International law in national courts, in: **Thomas M. Franck/ Gregory H. Fox (ed.),** International law decisions in national courts, (New York: Transnational Publishers 1996), p. 71

[13] 29 October 1987, in: Decisions vol. 2, p. 738

[14] 12 July 1994, in: International Law Reports, vol. 106 (1997), p. 320
Döris König, Putting an end to an endless constitutional debate? The decision of the Federal Constitutional Court on the "out of area" deployment of German Armed Forces, in: German Yearbook of International Law vol. 38 (1995) p.103
Robert Chr. Van Ooyen, Der Begriff des Politischen des Bundesverfassungsgerichts, (Berlin: Duncker& Humblot 2005), p.203

[15] Supreme Federal Court of Justice (Third Criminal Chamber) 27 February 1984, in: International Law Reports vol. 80 (1989), p. 389
Klaus Bockslaff/Michael Koch, The Tabatabai Case: The immunity of special envoys and the limits of judicial review, in: German Yearbook of International Law vol. 25 (1982), p.539
Jochen Abr. Frowein, Die Bindungswirkung von Akten der auswärtigen Gewalt insbesondere von rechtsfeststellenden Akten, in: **Jost Delbrück/Knut Ipsen/Dietrich Rauschning (ed.),** Recht im Dienst des Friedens, Festschrift für Eberhard Menzel zum 65. Geburtstag am 21.Januar 1976, (Berlin: Duncker & Humblot 1975), p.132
Wilfried Bolewski, Zur Bindung deutscher Gerichte an Äußerungen und Maßnahmen ihrer Regierung auf völkerrechtlicher Ebene. Ein Beitrag zur Verrechtlichung der Außenpolitik, jur. Diss. Marburg 1971

[16] **Volker Busse**, Der Kernbereich exekutiver Eigenverantwortung im Spannungsfeld der staatlichen Gewalt, in: Die Öffentliche Verwaltung, 1989, p. 45
Robert Chr. Van Ooyen, Der Begriff des Politischen, p.189

[17] **Daniel O. Burchardt,** Grenzen verfassungsgerichtlicher Erkenntnis, Zur Prozeduralität der Verfassungsnormativität, (Berlin: Duncker & Humblot 2004)
Rüdiger Wolfrum, Auswärtige Beziehungen und Verteidigungspolitik in: **Peter Badura/Horst Dreier,** Festschrift 50 Jahre Bundesverfassungsgericht, vol. 2, p. 693
Henning Schwarz, Die verfassungsgerichtliche Kontrolle der Außen- und Sicherheitspolitik. Ein Verfassungsvergleich Deutschland – USA, (Berlin: Duncker & Humblot 1995)
Michael Piazolo, Verfassungsgerichtsbarkeit und politische Fragen. Die Political Question Doktrin im Verfahren vor dem Bundesverfassungsgericht und dem Supreme Court der USA, (München: Verlag Ernst Vögel 1994)
Klaus Stern, Außenpolitischer Gestaltungsspielraum und verfassungsrecthliche Kontrolle. Das Bundesverfassungsgericht im Spannungsfeld zwischen Judicial Activism und Judicial Restraint, in: Nordrhein-Westfälische Verwaltungsblätter 7/ 1994, p. 241
Udo Di Fabio, Rechtsschutz im parlamentarischen Untersuchungsverfahren, (Berlin: Duncker & Humblot 1988)
Alard von Rohr, Kompetenz des Bundesverfassungsgerichts zur Überprüfung völkerrechtlicher Verträge, Diss, Kiel 1981
Folke Schuppert, Die verfassungsgerichtliche Kontrolle der Auswärtigen Gewalt, (Baden-Baden: Nomos 1973)

[18] **George Slyz,** p. 105

[19] **Thomas M. Franck,** Political questions/Judicial answers. Does the rule of law apply to foreign affairs?, (Princeton: Princeton University Press 1992), p.

III. National Courts and international relations

In contemporary international relations politics and law are closely linked and interdependent. They can no longer be seen as separate domains and treated as categorically distinct since many bridges have been constructed between international relations and international law. They coexist in a state of interdisciplinary cross-fertilization. International law and politics infuse and shape each other.

In an increasingly internationalized world, relations between and within various national communities tend to be governed more and more by international law. International Law is no longer the exclusive province of diplomats; it must evolve under the guidance of all "legal operators" and state organs charged with applying the law. These "domestic legal operators"[1] include the national judges. National courts are the vehicles through which international treaties and customary law that have not been independently incorporated into domestic legislation enter domestic legal systems. National courts, too, do not operate in an international vacuum; there is no judicial no-man's land. Due to growing globalization, no branch of government can afford to ignore the rest of the world. The dividing line between international and national law is disappearing. In a world where most aspects of life are becoming internationalized, domestic judges may be called upon to settle legal questions that may affect the external relations of their own state. National judges increasingly appear to show openness to international law, in particular for treaties and customary international law on the premise that international law, both customary and treaties, has its validity within the national legal system. International law changes how judges look at the world.

National courts show a remarkable understanding of the specific circumstances under which international negotiations are conducted and successfully try to find a balance between the requirements of national law and the demands of international relations.[2] The interpretation of treaties by the national judge is carried out in conformity with the principles of customary international law that have been formed on the subject and that are codified in the Vienna Convention on the Law of Treaties. The national judge should also make an effort to interpret the treaty as it would be interpreted by an international court, avoiding unilateral interpretation of the treaty or interpretation guided by national interests. Both treaty and customary law may be relevant to determining the rights of parties in litigation before national courts and consequently, much of the task of interpreting and implementing international norms is performed by domestic judges. According to practical experience, 90 % of international law issues envolving norms of positive law are dealt with in domestis courts.[3]

The decisions of national judges in relation to the application of international law are themselves part of the process of developing internatioinal customary law. Thus, their adjudication becomes an essential part of norm-implementation which is promoting compliance with international law.

This openness certainly facilitates the adaptation of the international legal order, also as interpreted by international tribunals.[4] This new role of the national judges in the application of international law will contribute to strengthen the respect for, as well as, the acceptability and the efficacy of international law in general and promote the "triumphant procession of the rule of law".[5] This could be an important step towards establishing and bestowing legitimacy upon an international rule of law.

The powerful phenomenon of globalization seems even to erode the traditional doctrines (Act of State doctrine, Political Question doctrine) formulated or embraced by national courts which empeded breaching the wall of sovereignty. National judges can now help to determine the new limits of sovereignty, which must leave enough room for the requirements, dynamics and impact of globalization[6], through their judicialization of international law.

Apart from the settlements of individual disputes, national courts offer a good, indeed sometimes the only opportunity for individuals to invoke international law and participate in the process of ensuring compliance with and shaping of international law. Along with emerging international tribunals this leads to a stronger legalization of international relations also through the national judiciary, thus remedying some of the institutional and structural imperfection in the international legal system. With the application of judicially discoverable and manageable (constitutional and international) standards a "new birth" of judicial review can be perceived. This juridical interpretation will also transform the relation between the law and international relations as well as the definition and functioning of the international system as such. An inter-judicial discourse can generate a new balance between systemic functional synergy and experimental tolerance for local sensibility.[7]

The internationalization of the law is thus complemented by an activation of the judiciary and a judicial empowerment to uphold constitutional as well as international law. The normative impregnation[8] of international relations as interpreted by national courts will change the nature of the interaction of all participants in the direction of the rule of law.

International law exists and operates in a social system with weak central institutions. Since the international legal system has no legislator competent to make universally applicable rules of law, the international and national courts can perform a role in effectuating international law. Domestic courts can help to overcome this structural weakness in the international legal system. Once individuals are permitted to raise questions of international law before a court these matters can be adjudicated according to international law. The national courts can potentially offer another complementary forum for judicial application of international law. They provide a reliable system of ensuring compliance with international norms. Together with international tribunals the courts of various countries afford the best structure for the development of a respected body of international law.

Apart from the dispute-deciding element adjudication also carries as a by-product a law-creating element; the courts become a legitimacy-building instrument for international law and for peaceful transformation of an international society. This activity by national courts shows real potential and great promise for the enhancement of international norms;[9] they can join in the process of international law-making.[10] These judicial organs can play an important role to provide authoritative interpretations of the state of the international law and to adjust the content of this law to the changing demands of the social community, thus preserbing the dynamic character of international law making.[11] Far from judicial activism this world-wide development could strengthen the confidence in international law as a value-oriented system.

The judicial empowerment of national courts could serve the following purposes:

- establish and protect fundamental rules and rights which go beyond national barriers forming the community standards of the international legal order,
- play a complementary role in the international law adjudication and enforcement processes including international law remedies and
- with due consideration to the domestic legal order- check on the abuse of power by other branches of state.

This perspective of a wider conception of sources and for a more progressive image of the nature of law in world affairs[12] conforms to Article 38 para. 1 lit. d of the International Court of Justice mentioning "judicial decision" as a source of international law.[13]

National courts are not only national institutions but also instruments of the international legal system and as such responsible for the development of norm-oriented behaviour. They guarantee the correlation between international law and national policy in international relations. Judges speak a sort of common language and use a similar rhetoric that is helpful in advancing understanding across borders. Such rhetoric establishes connections, traces similarities and creates intellectual frameworks. Their common language and convergent processes of decision-making can create inter-judicial synergies and pierce walls of sovereignty and set common standards.[14]

Since 1990, one can observe an increasing transnational judicial cooperation, especially among some constitutional courts leading to legal cross-fertilization of national judicial decisions and the emergence of "judicial comity".[15] Constitutional cross-fertilization is not only a function of globalization and the information revolution, it is also the driving force to promote the rule of law, to promote human rights and the administration of justice and, eventually, to build democracy through law. The lively interjudicial dialogue on international law possibly leading to interactive coordination between the adjucative bodies of the world community, particularly U.S., French, German and Japanese and international tribunals has brought about a series of cross-citations for different perspectives on similar issues (for example human rights) as it already exists among the courts of members of the Commonwealth. This global conversation of judges constitutes a new development. Where judges refer to foreign decisions as persuasive authority, constitutional cross-fertilization begins to evolve into an emerging global jurisprudence. As a result of this judicial globalization one can observe an increasingly global constitutional jurisprudence on common issues ranging from free speech to privacy rights and capital punishment.

The point that international sources are relevant to constitutional interpretation are relevant to the courts within a common legal enterprise[16] has been emphasized by the U.S. Supreme Court Justice Stephen Breyer[17]. He noted that judges everywhere face the same species of problems armed with the same species of legal instruments and that there is enormous value in any discipline of trying to learn from the similar experience of others.

Judicial dialogue is becoming a core issue of the general theme of globalization and the judiciary. It changes the judicial self-image as well as the working methods. Domestic courts will in their application of international law give more weight to persuasive than to binding authority. This phenomenon of high court judges entering into a global conversation by referring to and borrowing from each other has been described as judicial globalization.[18] In times of globalization, identical international legal problems and issues need similar legal responses. In the last decades there has been a general development towards convergence of many areas of the law presupposing a (more or less) homogeneous legal culture.

Transjudicial communication, enhanced by the internationalization of all domestic transactions, presupposes that the courts conceive themselves a autonomous governmental actors even beyond national borders and that they understand themselves to be engaged in a common judicial enterprise (transjudicialism)[19] of a world under law.[20]

Another example of growing mutual respect and understanding with ensuing active interaction is the fact that the German Constitutional Court – since 1992- provides an official translation of its decisions in English.[21] This becomes relevant since international and foreign national courts are relying more and more on the decisions of (other) national courts as a display of comity or mutual respect.[22] As judges are globalizing as well, their transjudicial relations contribute to a foundation for a global community of law[23] and the gradual construction of an integrated global legal system.

In an attempt to strengthen the respect for international law eminent academics of the Ninth Commission of the Institute of International Law[24] under the Rapporteur Benedetto Conforti have adopted in 1993 a Resolution on "The activities of national judges and the international relations of their state".[25] Their main conclusions are:

- The national judge should be free to autonomously evaluate international facts and to autonomously settle every question of international law. Naturally, the Executive should retain its prerogative to intervene as amicus curiae for the purpose of cooperating.
- The ascertainment of international facts made by the Executive should constitute prima facie evidence of the existence of these facts themselves. But the last word should be with the judge.
- The national judge cannot review conduct of the Executive that is contrary to customary law when the Executive shows that its conduct is justified by an adequate opinio necessitatis and therefore aims at contributing to the transformation of the customary law in force.

The fulfillment of international law is found in the internal legal systems of states. Their domestic legal operators are implementing international law in a concrete and continuous way. Thus, compliance with international law relies not so much on enforcement mechanisms available at the international level, but rather on the resolve of domestic legal operators to use and exploit the mechanisms provided by municipal law.[26]

On the basis of these suggestions the national judiciary should be bold enough to live up to its democratic responsibility to legally guide foreign affairs through international law, thus securing the rule of law and strengthening the process of constitutionalization of diplomacy in defence of international common values (solidarist conception of international law) and normative relations. Another consequence could be a process of harmonization and convergence of national legal systems.[27] The effect of legal internationalization or even globalization has been to introduce, through the national margin of appreciation, both recognition of the diversity and harmonization of the pluralism of legal systems with the possible convergence into a common legal order. The existing pluralism and legitimate difference, whereby judges acknowledge the validity of a wide variety of different approaches to the same legal problems operates within a framework of common fundamental values, such as recognition of the necessity of judicial independence and basic due process.[28]

The role and responsability of judges who participate in the reciprocal generation of norms and in the emergence of a rule community (global international law) has to be reevaluated since the function of the courts in the state framework is expanding in the field of the interpretation of international law. Their increased self-assurance and authority can lead to a new assertive role and can eventually foster the credibility of the judiciary in the development of the rule of law. With such a shift of power from the executive branch to the judiciary as "enforcers" of international law there would practically be no danger of juridification of politics or of politicizing the judiciary[29], but rather a significant contribution to the body of international law.

References

1 **Benedetto Conforti,** International law and the role of the domestic legal systems, (Dordrecht: Martinus Nijhoff Publishers 1993), p.1

2 **Uwe Kischel,** The state as a non-unitary actor: The role of the judicial branch in international negotiations, in: Archiv des Völkerrechts vol. 39 (2001), p.268

3 **Christian Tomuschat** in his introduction to a conference on "The Role of Domestic Courts in the Enforcement of International Law" at the Humboldt University, Berlin, on January 17, 2007.

4 **Thomas Buergenthal,** International tribunals and national courts: The internationalization of domestic adjudication, in: **Ulrich Beyerlin/ Michael Bothe/Rainer Hofmann/Ernst-Ulrich Petersmann (ed.),** Recht zwischen Umbruch und Bewahrung. Völkerrecht – Europarecht – Staatsrecht. Festschrift für Rudolf Bernhardt, (Berlin: Springer 1995), p. 687
Theodor Schweisfurth/ Ralf Alleweldt, The position of international law in the domestic legal orders of central and eastern European countries, in: German Yearbook of International Law vol. 40 (1997), p.164

5 **Philip Kunig,** Völkerrecht als öffentliches Recht – Ein Glasperlenspiel, in: **Albrecht Randelzhofer/Rupert Scholz/Dieter Wilke (ed.),** Gedächtnisschrift für Eberhard Grabitz, (München: Beck 1995) p. 325

Stefan Kadelbach/ Thomas Kleinlein, Überstaatliches Verfassungsrecht, in: Archiv des Völkerrechts vol. 44 (2006) p. 235 (265)
Sigrid Boysen, Kriegsverbrechen im Diskurs nationaler Gerichte, in: Archiv des Völkerrechts vol. 44 (2006) p.363 (378)

6 **Georg Nolte,** Sovereignty as responsibility?, in: American Society of Internnational Law Proceedings 2005, p. 389

7 **Thomas M. Franck/Gregory H. Fox (ed.),** International law decisions in national courts (New York: Transnational Publishers 1996), p. 11

8 **Robert Badinter,** Le gouvernement des juges vu par les juges? in: **Séverine Brondel/ Norbert Foulquier/Luc Heuschling (ed.),** Gouvernement des juges et démocratie, (Paris: Publications de la Sorbonne 2001), p.289

9 **Eyal Benvenisti,** Judges and foreign affairs: A comment on the Institut de Droit International's resolution on "The activities of national courts and the international relations of their state", in: European Journal of International Law, vol 5 (1994) no. 3, p. 423

10 **Michel Troper/Otto Pfersmann,** Existe-t-il un concept de gouvernement des juges? in: **Séverine Brondel/Norbert Foulquier/Luc Heuschling,** p. 21

11 **Andrea Bianchi,** The Act of State: the state of the act. Judicial interpretation and human rights enforcement, in: **Marcelo G. Kohen,** Promoting justice, human rights and conflict resolution through international law. Liber Amicorum Lucius Caflisch, (Leiden: Martinus Nijhoff Publishers 2007), p. 129 (149)

12 **Richard A. Falk,** The role of domestic courts in the international legal order, (Syracuse: Syracuse University Press 1964), p. 3

13 **Jörg Menzel,** Einleitung: Völkerrecht als Recht vor Gerichten, in: **Jörg Menzel/ Tobias Pierlings/Jeannine Hoffmann (ed.),** Völkerrechtsprechung. Ausgewählte Entscheidungen zum Völkerrecht in Retrospektive, (Tübingen: Mohr Siebeck 2005), p. 33
R.Y. Jennings, The judiciary, international and national, and the development of international law, in: International and Comparative Law Quaterly, vol. 45 (1996), p. 1 (3)

14 **John B. Attanasio,** Rapporteur's Overview and Conclusions: of Sovereignty, Globalization and Courts, in: **Thomas M. Franck/Gregory H. Fox (ed.)**, International law decisions in national courts (New York: Transnational Publishers 1996), p. 373

15 **Anne-Marie Slaughter,** Judicial globalization, in: Virginia Journal of International Law vol. 40 (2000) p. 1103

16 **Daniel Bodansky,** The use of international sources in constitutional opinion, in: Georgia Journal of International and Comparative Law, vol. 32 (2004), p. 421

17 **Stephen Breyer,** The Supreme Court and the New International Law, Address to the American Society of International Law, 97th Annual Meeting, Washington, D.C., April 4, 2003
(No author), Developments in the law; international criminal law. VI. The international judicial dialogue: when domestic constitutional courts join the conversation, in: Harvard Law Review, vol. 114 (2000/2001), p. 1943 (2049)

[18] **Carl Baudenbacher,** Judicial Globalization: New development or old wine in new bottles?, in: Texas International Law Journal, vol. 38 (2003), p. 505

[19] **Sandra Day O'Connor,** Keynote Address at the Proceedings of the 96th Annual Meeting of the American Society of International Law, March 16, 2002 (Washington: The American Society of International Law 2002) p. 348
Karen Knop, Here and there: International law in domestic courts, in: New York University Journal of International Law and Politics, vol. 32 (1999/2000), p. 501 (505)

[20] **Anne-Marie Slaughter,** A typology of transjudicial communications, in: **Thomas M. Franck/Gregory H. Fox (ed),** p. 37

[21] Decisions of the Federal Constitutional Court – Federal Republic of Germany (Baden-Baden: Nomos 1992)

[22] **Mohammed Bedjaoui,** The reception by national courts of decisions of international tribunals, in: **Thomas M. Franck/Gregory H. Fox (ed.),** International law decisions in national courts (New York: Transnational Publishers 1996), p. 21
Sandra Day O'Connor, Federalism and free nations, in: **Thomas M. Franck/Gregory H. Fox (ed),** p, 13 (19): "The principles of limited judicial power teach us do defer to the policy judgment of the political branches, especially in the conduct of foreign affairs. At the same time, our Court (U.S. Supreme Court), consistent with our constitutional ideals, has recognized the dictate of international law and observed the comity accorded to the opinions of foreign courts. I hope that this balanced tradition will serve our Court well as it is asked to define the role of domestic courts in the international legal regime."

[23] **William W. Burke-White,** A community of courts: Toward a system of international criminal law enforcement, in: Michigan Journal of International Law, vol. 24 (2002/2003) p. 1 (84,85)

[24] Bernhardt, Caportorti, Collins, Gannagé, van Hecke, Lauterpacht, Lowenfeld, Mann, Marotta Rangel, Mbaye, Ni Zhengyu, Palolillo, Sahovic, Seidl-Hohenveldern, De Visscher, Wildhaber
Yearbook of the Institute of International Law vol. 65 (1993), part 1, p. 327,

[25] **Eyal Benvenisti,** p. 423
See also The International Law Association, Reports of the 66th Conference (1994) p. 326, 67th Conference (1996) p. 570 and 68th Conference (1998) p. 659

[26] **Benedetto Conforti,** p. 8

[27] **Mireille Delmas-Marty/Marie-Laure Izorche,** Marge nationale d'appréciation et internationalisation du droit: réflexions sur la validité formelle d'un droit commun pluraliste, in: McGill Law Journal, vol.46 (2001) p. 923

[28] **Anne-Marie Slaughter,** A new world order, (Princeton: Princeton University Press 2004), p. 69
Karen Knop, p. 501
Markus Kotzur, Weltrecht ohne Weltstaat – die nationale (Verfassungs-)Gerichtsbarkeit als Motor völkerrechtlicher Konstitutionalisierungsprozesse?, in: Die Öffentliche Verwaltung 2002, p. 195 (201)

[29] **François Guizot,** Des conspirations et de la justice politique (Paris: Fayard 1984), p. 170

Conclusions and outlook: Diplomacy as an instrument of globalized societies

Globalization is a process among states leading to a globalized international order as well as a domestic process of change within states. Globalization does not make the state as such disappear or obsolete but is a guiding element of change in the functionality of the state.

The ongoing shifts in global economic and political power and the appearance of new participants in world politics foreshadow structural changes in our world – a world characterized by greater distribution of power as well as new opportunities and uncertainties. As history testifies, tectonic shifts in power usually create volatility in the international system, even if such volatility is short-lived, and soon is replaced by new emerging structures. Good statecraft demands adjustments to such shifts with the aim to create a new balance of political and economic power in the world. The central challenge is to promote cooperative approaches that can tackle today's security, energy, territorial, environmental, developmental and history issues to the benefit of humankind (bonum commune humanitatis).[1] Global public goods are an often ignored but enormously important aspect of multilateralism. The lodestar should be the outreach of multilateralism, its consensus-building potential and the observance of the principles of the rule of law ("Rechtsstaat") both at the national and international level.

Whereas private authority in foreign affairs generally escapes the legal system of judicial review, the public authority of the state is principally subject to public international law in its foreign policy decisions by the executive. But its legal control in foreign courts is guided and limited by the international regime of state immunity and in national courts by the judicial restraint of national judges. The national judiciary should be bold enough to live up to its democratic responsibility to legally guide foreign affairs through international law, thus securing the rule of law and strengthening the process of constitutionalization of diplomacy in defence of international common values and normative relations. Thus, the role of judges who participate in the reciprocal generation of norms and in the emergence of a rule community (global international law) has to be revaluated.

The fact that there are new participants in the playing field can only be welcomed. The contributions by civil society and the non-governmental organizations are of particular importance. New non-state participants have an increasing impact on decision-making in contemporary society. In fact, these participants contribute significantly to strengthening the system of governance both at the national and international level due to a new tripartism with fuller involvement of civil society and business in intergovernmental processes.

The new governance challenges transcend the various levels linking the local with the national, regional and global levels. As a result, they require cooperation among institutions across levels and issue-areas, i.e. multi-level governance. Moreover, states as well as international organizations are less and less able to cope with theses challenges. They require intensified cooperation between public and private participants including transnational companies and NGOs: From the cooperations of governments with networks of other public and private participants (governance by and with government) to self-regulation and self-coordination by non-state participants or civil society (governance without government).These new modes and innovative patterns of new governance must also lead to adjustments in constitutional provisions to ensure legitimacy and accountability as well as the rule of law.

Accountability in global governance can only be reached by balancing the needs for transparency and openness with the challenge for efficacy.

The interdependence of global developments and the complexity of resulting problems involve also a process of societal denationalization which reduced the significance of national borders and poses a challenge to the efficacy of national policies.[2]

The reciprocal dependencies and vulnerabilities need and justify a new strategy of corresponding political denationalization in the form of global governance ("Weltordnungspolitik"). Political denationalization describes a process whereby the role of governance increases beyond the nation state relative to national forms of governance.

This needs the cooperation of state and non-state participants and new forms of common problem-solving from the local to the global level. The nation-state is losing its undisputed role as the hub of political action. The architecture of politics is undergoing a radical change. Though the nation-states are no longer the only participants because many different actors are taking part, the nation-state nevertheless continues to be the major participant in international affairs.

One very often hears the argument that these participants and, in particular, powerful transnational companies undermine the authority of national governments (as the self-determined power to rule in matters internal and external). But this genuine challenge actually only leads to the very concept of shared political sovereignty[3]: a redistributed division of labour and responsibility between state, economy and social organizations.

The increasing privatization of public authority does not necessarily lead to an alienation of sovereignty or a democratic deficit but it could also eventually bring about a strengthening of state institutions provided it is accompanied by popular acceptance and a certain degree of state control. These effects of globalization can even become a driving force to a new understanding of statehood.[4]

In a system of global governance authority (in the form of sovereignty and ensuing responsibility) is shared among government and non-government participants in a transnational network.[5] This could even create an effective new world order. Global governance therefore is not merely a foreign-policy concept but with the blurring of the distinction between domestic and foreign policy (intermestic affairs) it becomes a project for reorganizing politics at every level of action.

In discoursive interaction between pluralistic participants and structures sovereignty as responsibility is continuously disaggregated and recomposed. This shared sovereignty does not mean the deprivation of the state's internal monopoly on power since the basic elements (core tasks) of statehood cannot be abdicated and simply entrusted to any other body than institutions of a sovereign state: such as exercise of legislative authority, national security, law enforcement. But it calls on the national-state to forgo a measure of (traditional) sovereignty so that global problems can be tackled collectively. This is to be accepted as a supplementary or at times complementary contribution to the components of a modern democratic society. Global governance therefore implies a new understanding of politics and operational sovereignty. One of the principal functions of sovereignty today is to develop cooperation between all participants in globalized relations. The need for cooperation entails a relinquishing of traditional sovereignty and leads to a system of shared sovereignty coupled with a reallocation and transformation of power to other layers and participants within a multi-governance network (capability to shape global dynamics collectively or individually, in vertical or horizontal structures). Thus, the notion of state sovereignty has been redefined by the forces of globalization and international cooperation and may be interpreted in an newly adapted and extended way.[6]

In the process of globalization, apart from the concept of sovereignty also that of subsidiarity is under review.[7] Whereas sovereignty is in its core a legal concept the principle of subsidiarity is primarily a societal and political concept however with normative relevance. "Subsidium" means help and support and the principle of subsidiarity therefore constitutes different forms of supplementary support starting out from an individual sphere and going up to local, regional, state and global levels. International solidarity, coordination and cooperation in the context of communitarianism will have to respect the principle of subsidiarity: political intervention and regulation only as much as necessary, but as little as possible.

Subsidiarity remains a principal paradigm of global governance.

In the search of common problem-solving strategies in cooperation or co-authorship with societal groups a sense of community is developing around a common life world ("gemeinsame Lebenswelt"). Politics is thus coming back into society. Outlines are emerging of a network society, in which non-state institutions and transnational companies also have to assume responsibility for the development of the global community.

In this context also non-governmental organizations take up a supplementary authority as participants in the formative process:

- They can operate in problem-areas which the state has not addressed properly – or has not yet addressed at all.
- They can be formed in order to keep the state out of particular problem-areas; the state can then limit its activities to that of monitoring the results.
- They can monitor and effect adjustments to state intervention.
- Finally, they can establish themselves as important players in world society; groups concerned with developments, human rights, and the environment help to shape an international public. Though they often – justifiably – represent particular interests they can contribute to uphold common values.

Global interdependences make international cooperation imperative and cast into doubt the rationality and morality of one-sided nation-state politics of self-interest that is geared to maximizing the benefits to oneself. A realistic redefinition of self-interests in times of globalization should also recognize and prioritize universally shared values and principles of action which form the global common good.

In future, common efforts at global problem-solving should be seen as mutual intervention and coordinated activities from the local to the global level. This search for common values is focussed on the guiding principle of communitarianism. It is this cooperative communitarianism which also provides a new formative aspect to sovereignty. It combines the cosmopolitan interests of state, society and business. This network-like-system presupposes a minimum of trust, fairness and understanding of the "One World" concept for collective survival. This strategy eventually converges in the production of a positive identity in the global arena.

The hallmark of a global community may be found in the appropriation or definition of common assets and the upgrading of common interests. These globalized goods are manifold and form our common life world:

- material (common resources): such as the deep bed of the high sea,
- territorial: such as certain areas of space (both material and territorial are defined as "Common Heritage of Mankind"),
- functional: such as certain aspects of collective security or
- spiritual: internationally defined human rights or ecological norms represent common spiritual assets where states can no more assert their exclusive sovereignty, even within their territory, than they could over areas of space which extend above their air-space.

By definition, these assets are not subject to selfish use but are objects of cooperation for the welfare of the common good (common weal). Due to the global interdependence the regulation and protection of these common assets can only be managed through communitarian consensus or distributive compromise on the basis of underlying shared principles and a common knowledge and global responsibilities.

The new strategy of global governance as response to the trend of globalization occasionally leads to the dichotomy between democracy and legitimacy on one side and efficacy on the other. In a destabilizing world when and where state functions and responsibilities are fragile or failing the democratic political processes also come under threat. Under these circumstances (temporary) effective problem-solving through non-state actors (NGOs, TNCs) becomes a supplementary option of global good governance. Thus, efficacy can have a stabilizing and regulatory effect in the emergence of denationalized governance structures which can eventually improve both social welfare and democracy in the face of societal denationalization. This functionality of an efficient and sustainable problem-solving capacity provides the new democratic legitimacy[8] to global good governance which can also help to dissolve the dichotomy between law and politics.

What is it that can hold all these changes, structures and new partners in globalized relations together?

What can serve as the lubricating device for all participants on the international scene?

Diplomacy has passed the test of time and adversity in the conduct of international relations among states and other subjects of international law. Diplomacy is here to stay: The question is only, by whom, at what level, how and to what ends it will be carried out. It has shown its remarkable ability and resilience to adapt to change rather than wither away. It has been accepted and practised by all forms of government whether democratic or autocratic. Through experience and teaching it has been passed down to modern times.

International education can transport these norms, rules and practices to the new participants in globalized relations.

Diplomacy has moved from an art form to a management tool reflecting the growing interdependence between globalized societies. Nowadays, diplomacy is not only a policy instrument but also an international process of social relationships adapted by the civil society in the contemporary global system.

Not only do international organizations act diplomatically but as has been shown by NGOs and transnational corporations they too are eager to integrate themselves in the diplomatic culture absorbing the structures and making use of them for their own causes. Diplomacy remains a highly relevant process in contemporary world politics and a useful instrument for a wide range of global participants.

Human touch diplomacy and especially protocol as behavioural guidance facilitate through their internationally accepted structures the interaction and eventually help to create a sense of international community among the participants.

In the ongoing tectonic shifts through globalization, diplomacy can provide the necessary structural stability if its tools are extended to the transnational and intermestic areas. Under the primacy of reason, globalized societies are the fertile ground for the renaissance and rejuvenation of preventive diplomacy in order to structure their privatization and at the same time to slow down if not prevent their creeping militarization. Modern diplomacy, its procedures and global dynamics can thus contribute to the search for a new world order. New diplomacy should be essentially a collaborative effort and responsibility by all participants in globalized societies (state and non-state, governmental and civil societal) for the broader project of promoting values and ideas. Joining public and private resources in synergetic and symbiotic relationships will foster the overall problem solving capacity and increase societal participation in the processes of degovernmentalization of governance and privatization of globalized relations. To activate this common value basis is the collective challenge of the future.

The diplomatic potential with its skills and ingenuity in particular circumstances has to be adapted to the political, military, and economic changes of globalization.[9] We need to revive diplomacy in order to strengthen lasting international peace.

References

[1] **Alfred Verdroß**, Der klassische Begriff des "bonum commune" und seine Entfaltung zum "bonum commune humanitatis", in: Österreichische Zeitschrift für Öffentliches Recht und Völkerrecht 1977, p. 143.

[2] **Michael Zürn**, Globalization and Global Governance: From Societal to Political Denationalization in: **Reinhard C. Meier-Walser / Peter Stein**, Globalisierung und Perspektiven internationaler Verantwortung, (München: Saur Verlag 2003), p. 422

[3] **Hubert Védrine,** Refonder la politique étrangère française, in: Le Monde diplomatique, décembre 2000, p. 3
Hubert Védrine, Les Cartes de la France à l'heure de la mondialisation, (Paris: Fayard 2000)

[4] **Jean-François Bayart,** Le gouvernement du monde. Une critique politique de la globalisation, (Paris: Fayard 2004), p. 123,
Zaki Laïdi, Penser la mondialisation, (Paris: Flammarion 2002)
Martin Shaw, Theory of the global state. Globality as unfinished revolution (Cambridge: Cambridge University Press 2000), p.270
Martin van Creveld, The rise and decline of the state, (Cambridge: Cambridge University Press 1999), p. 415

[5] **Anne-Marie Slaughter,** A new world order, (Princeton: Princeton University Press 2004), p. 270

[6] **Montserrat Cuchillo,** From sovereignty to decentralization, European integration and global governance, in: **David J. Eaton (ed.),** The end of sovereignty? A transatlantic perspective, (Hamburg: LIT Verlag 2006), p. 97 (119)
Mireille Delmas-Marty, Trois défis pour un droit mondial, (Paris: Editions du Seuil 1998), p. 175

[7] **Herbert Schambeck**, Subsidiarität und Souveränität in Zeiten der Globalisierung, In: The Governance of Globalisation, (Vatican: The Pontifical Academy of Social Sciences 2004), acta 9, p. 117

[8] **Karl-Peter Sommermann,** Demokratie als Herausforderung des Völkerrechts, in: **Pierre-Marie Dupuy/Bardo Fassbender/Malcolm N. Shaw/Karl-Peter Sommermann (ed.),** Common Values in International Law.Essays in Honour of Christian Tomuschat, (Kehl: N.P. Engel Verlag 2006), p. 1051

[9] **Barry H. Steiner,** Diplomacy and international theory, in: Review of International Studies, vol. 30 (2004), p. 493 (508)

Printing: Krips bv, Meppel
Binding: Stürtz, Würzburg